The Medieval Housewife
& other women of the Middle Ages

Toni Mount

AMBERLEY

To the memory of my Nan, Amy Thomas, and my Mum, Joyce Botting, both long-suffering, hard-working housewives who held down numerous part-time jobs to make ends meet, yet succeeded in being dedicated and loving mothers.

To the unsung domestic heroines of every generation.

First published 2014

Amberley Publishing
The Hill, Stroud
Gloucestershire, GL5 4EP

www.amberley-books.com

British Library Cataloguing in Publication Data.
A catalogue record for this book is available from the British Library.

ISBN 978 1 4456 4370 0 (paperback)
ISBN 978 1 4456 4402 8 (ebook)

Typesetting and Origination by Amberley Publishing.
Printed in Great Britain.

Contents

A straight-laced woman at the Battle of
Bosworth re-enactment, 2014. (Pat Patrick)

The Role of Medieval Women

More has been written about medieval women in the last twenty years than in the two whole centuries before that. Female authors of the medieval period, like the Frenchwoman Christine de Pisan, and the Englishwomen Julian of Norwich and Margery Kempe, have been rediscovered and new editions and translations of their works produced. Queens are no longer thought of as merely decorative brood mares for their royal husbands and have merited their own biographies; examples of some of the most recent include *The Last Medieval Queens* by J. L. Laynesmith, *Elizabeth Woodville* by David Baldwin and *Queens Consort: England's Medieval Queens* by Lisa Hilton. Tax records and manorial court rolls have revealed the names of thousands of ordinary women, while fascinating human insights can be gained from women's wills and letters.

From the London Borough records of 1281, we learn of this ruling on the wearing of fur:

> It is proved and commanded that no woman of the City shall from henceforth go to market or in the king's highway, out of her house, with a hood furred with other than lambskin or rabbitskin, on pain of losing her hood to the use of the sheriffs, save only those ladies who wear furred capes; the hoods of these may have such furs as they may think fit. And this because regratresses, nurses and other servants and women of loose life dress themselves excessively and wear hoods furred with great vair and miniver in guise of good ladies.

However, administrative records were compiled for financial or legal reasons and the women who appear in them represent just a small fraction of the total female population. Therefore, historians know far more about widows who held property and who enjoyed legal independence than they know about wives whose legal identity was overshadowed by that of their husbands. More is revealed about women when they come up against the law, such as female ale brewers, or 'brewsters'. For much of the medieval period, brewsters were fined regularly for bad practice, but hardly anything is known about women who worked as laundresses and seamstresses, since these crafts were never formally regulated. Any kind of record, read alone, can only give us one view of the total picture. Wills written by women reveal fascinating insights about their piety and

Above left: Wife making medicine for her sick husband. (MS Royal 15 D I f.18, British Library – The Blinding of Tobit, *Bible Historiale of Edward IV*, Bruges, 1470–9)

Above right: Mother and baby at the Battle of Tewkesbury re-enactment, 2014. (Pat Patrick)

personal relationships towards the end of life but say nothing of their attitudes and situation at other times during their lives.

Being female, wives were primarily responsible for managing the household and caring for the children, and this work (being women's work) was less highly regarded than the work done by men. Women of all social classes were depicted, not only as physically weaker, but weaker rationally and morally, likely to lead men astray. Generally, they had a restricted choice of occupation and fewer opportunities for education and the acquisition of property than men in the same social group. The material well-being of women was determined by their social class, affecting housing, diet, clothing and behaviour. Although aristocratic women enjoyed fewer rights than their brothers, they did have greater access to education, property and political power than any peasant woman.

The opportunities available to a woman varied, not only according to her social class, but also to the stage she had reached in her life. Daughters, whatever their rank in society, were legally under the control and authority of their fathers or guardians. Wives were subjected to the power and authority of their husbands, although some, like Eleanor de Montfort who was reprimanded by a friar for 'marital insubordination', did not necessarily give in quietly. Usually only widows had any measure of legal independence and this only applied to those with some degree of wealth, like Dame Elizabeth Cook (for her will, see chapter 3). However, women of

A medieval woman at the Loxwood Joust, West Sussex, 2014. (Glenn Mount)

lower ranks might also enjoy some degree of freedom at other stages of their lives. By the fourteenth and fifteenth centuries, the daughters of labourers and artisans often left home at the age of twelve or thirteen to work for others as servants and apprentices. Away from direct parental control, they were far freer to choose their own marriage partner than a young aristocratic girl whose parents regarded her marriage as a means to consolidate their property or expand their network of allies.

Wives, in both countryside and town, who supplemented the family income by brewing, spinning or selling produce, could sometimes spend their earnings as they wished, despite their husband's legal authority. However, these same women, once widowed, might choose or be required to live with a married son or daughter and so relinquish some degree of independence. The legal independence that widowhood brought was of little value if the widow herself had few, if any, resources at her disposal.

In the past, historians have tended to look at what women could *not* do. Now we regard women as capable and independent people, able to cope with tricky circumstances, we can consider what rights and opportunities women *did* enjoy – a case of seeing the glass half full, rather than half empty. This book looks at the lives of medieval women in a positive light using contemporary sources, such as the classics of medieval literature written by both men and women, wills, personal letters, household accounts and legal documents, in order to help us understand and visualise their roles.

Medieval Housewives

Have you ever wondered what life was like for the ordinary housewife in the Middle Ages? How did she manage the daily round of cooking, cleaning, shopping and looking after her husband and children? How do we know?

One of the best sources of information we have is a book written by a man previously known to us as the Menagier de Paris or the Goodman of Paris, but now identified as Guy de Montigny (thanks to research by Nicola Crossley-Holland), in which he described all the domestic duties in detail for his new young wife. He was in his sixties and she was an orphan of good birth aged about fifteen. This age difference was not considered outrageous in the 1390s when he was writing; in fact, such a marriage was thought to be a good match for both parties as the elderly husband got a new lease of life and the young bride got a ready-made household and a husband who had achieved a good station in life. Although it was usually the case that a woman's first husband was selected by her family or guardians, once widowed, the choice of a second spouse was hers to make, so if the husband was elderly, she may not have to wait too long for the man of her choosing. The bride in this case, being an orphan, had had no mother to instruct her in the arts of housewifery, but her husband had been married before so knew exactly what he wanted in a wife.

A medieval woman at the Battle of Bosworth re-enactment, 2014. (Pat Patrick)

Guy tells us in his prologue that since her 'youth excuses unwisdom', he will write this book of instruction for her, saying magnanimously,

I would that you know how to give good will and honour and service in great measure and abundance more than is fit for me, either to serve another husband, if you have one, after me, or to teach greater wisdom to your daughters, friends or others, if you list and have such need. For the more you know the greater honour will be yours and the greater praise will therefore be unto your parents and to me and to others about you, by whom you have been nurtured.

In other words, her excellence as a housewife in the future will reflect the very high standards of his instructions. Guy's book is written in three sections. The first, he says, is to instruct her in how to gain the love of God and the salvation of her soul, to win the love of her husband and to give her the peace experienced through marriage. The second section tells her how to run the household and tend the garden. The third and final section, which he never quite finished, describes suitable pastimes and amusements, how to feed and fly a falcon and a selection of riddles – an odd assortment of topics, designed to keep a young lady out of mischief. Incidentally, although this book was written by a Frenchman, there was even less difference between a French household and an English one then than there is now and only his list of suitable and convenient Parisian butchers and poulterers could not have applied to an English housewife of the same period. His examples of perfect wives, such as patient Griselda, would have been familiar in England as the story of Griselda is one of Geoffrey Chaucer's *Canterbury Tales*.

Of greatest importance to the Goodman of Paris were the instructions on 'how to be careful and thoughtful of your husband's person' and 'how to prepare viands', seen below.

LOVING YOUR HUSBAND

Wherefore love your husband's person carefully, and I pray you keep him in clean linen, for 'tis your business, and because the trouble and care of outside affairs lieth with men, so must husbands take heed, and go and come, and journey hither and thither, in rain and wind, in snow and hail, now drenched, now dry, now sweating, now shivering, ill-fed, ill-lodged, ill-warmed and ill-bedded. And naught harmeth him, because he is upheld by the hope that he hath of the care which his wife will take of him on his return, and of the ease, the joys and the pleasures she will do him … to be unshod before a good fire, to have his feet washed and fresh shoes and hose, to be given good food and drink, to be well served and well looked after, well bedded in white sheets and nightcaps, well covered with good furs, and assuaged with other joys and desports, privities, loves and secrets whereof I am silent. And the next day fresh shirts and garments. Certes, fair sister, such services make a man love and desire to return home and to see his goodwife, and to be distant with others.

So, what has changed in 600 years? The following illustration shows why the

Bed scene. (MS Harley 4425 f.122v, British Library – Venus, Vulcan and Mars, *Roman de la Rose*, Bruges, 1490–1500)

Goodman only required 'white sheets and nightcaps': folk generally slept naked.

The medieval author Christine de Pisan gives her own version of how to treat a husband in her book, *The Treasure of the City of Ladies*. She is talking to the wives of well-to-do merchants who have not been kind, with a view to their ultimate inheritance of their husbands' businesses when they die. While awaiting this happy outcome, the wife should

> … Administer the household with great care and prudence and be able to instruct the servants in the proper performance of their tasks. Her children should be well taught, unspoiled and not too noisy: their nurses should keep them clean and well behaved. The house should be so attractive and peaceful that the husband would always be happy to return home with friends to be entertained, such occasions allowing her to show off the handsome linen she had sewn and embroidered herself. The wife should not only go to mass early and say her prayers devoutly, but should ensure that nothing was ever wasted that might be given to the poor, and share her own meat and wine with them.

This paragon of virtue would not only keep on good terms with all of her neighbours but would not talk too much either.

CARE OF CLOTHES AND THE HOME

The Goodman of Paris and his wife were quite well off; he instructs her how to hire, fire and keep the servants in order and it is likely they were well provided with bedding and suchlike. For a glimpse of the likely range of household goods for an English merchant's household, we have the will of Ellen Langwith, the widow of a fairly wealthy London tailor, drawn up in 1480. Ellen, having no heirs, leaves the bulk of her possessions to John Brown, her one-time apprentice and brother of her serving maid. John is to have

> The best feather bed and bolster, 2 blankets, a mattress, 2 pairs of large sheets, 2 down pillows with pillow beres [cases], a stained [dyed] tester and curtains, a coverlet of tapestry work and a set of hangings of green buckrum.

That just covers the bedding; more of Ellen Langwith's will later. All this bedding had to be kept clean and sweet. In fine weather, the sheets could be washed, being spread to dry and bleach in the sun on the grass or draped along the hedgerows. However, all the heavy woollen blankets, fur coverlets etc. also had to be kept fresh and, most importantly, free of moths, bed bugs, fleas and suchlike. The Goodman of Paris informs his wife of the best methods of keeping both bedding and clothing free of undesirable inhabitants:

> In summer, scatter the chamber with alder leaves and the fleas will get caught therein. Item. I have heard tell that if at night you set one or two trenchers of bread covered with birdlime and put them about the chamber with a lighted candle set in the midst of each, the fleas will come and get stuck thereto. As for furs and garments in which there be fleas, fold and shut them up straitly in a chest or press bound with straps so the said fleas are without light and air and kept imprisoned, then they will perish and die at once.

The Goodman also instructs his wife in the removal of grease spots and stains from clothes, using vinegar and white wine, which actually works. For the better off, garments could be made of silk, velvet, damask, fur or other fabrics that could not be washed. In this event, John Russell, in his *Boke of Nurture*, gives clear instructions:

> In the warderobe ye must muche entende besily the robes to kepe well and also to brusche them clenly; with the ende of a soft brusche ye brusche them clenly, and yet ouer moche bruschynge werethe cloth lyghtly. Lett neuer wollyn cloth ne furre passe a seuennyght to be unbrosshen and shakyn, tend therto aright, for moughtes [moths] be redy euer in them to gendur and alight; therfore to drapery and skynnery euer haue ye a sight.

Clothes that could be washed, like shirts, shifts and undergarments, were made of linen and usually home stitched and embroidered, sometimes even the linen fabric itself was home spun and woven. Washing actually improved the fabric, bleaching and softening it the more it was washed.

The author as a medieval housewife at Bolton Castle, Wensleydale, North Yorkshire (Glenn Mount)

The tailor's widow, Ellen Langwith, bequeathed to Mistress Bowyer of Northampton 'a shorte gowne of blak medley [probably a wool mixture] furred with white lambe' and to her cousin, Mistress Bounesley of Nottingham, 'my best gowne of blue furred with martrons [marten fur]'; 'my girdull of blue silk harneised [decorated] with silvere and gilt' was bequeathed to Mary Jakes, a draper's wife. This kind of clothing would have to be kept in good shape by brushing, shaking out, regular airing and storing among lavender, dried rose petals and herbs to keep them sweet-smelling and, hopefully, moth free. Incidentally, clothes were often hung up in the garde-robe – a word which has the same meaning as our 'wardrobe', but the garde-robe was also a medieval toilet. They believed that moths hated the stink as much as people did and stayed away, thus their robes were guarded. So they had even more reason for using lavender and rose petals before wearing their Sunday best to church.

BUYING AND WEARING CLOTHES

Clothes were so expensive and highly regarded that even the queen's exchequer accounts of Isabella, queen of Edward II, show that she had the worn-out hems of her gowns replaced, rather than pay for entirely new gowns. This was at the beginning of the fourteenth century but, by the mid-fifteenth century, well-to-do people like the Pastons were sending their menfolk to London with lengthy shopping lists:

A young maiden at the Loxwood Joust, West Sussex, 2014. (Glenn Mount)

Buy me 3 yards of purple camlet at 4s a yard; a bonnet of deep murrey [mulberry colour] at 2s 4d; a hose cloth of yellow kersey of an ells length which should cost 2s; a girdle of plunkett [a blue-grey colour] ribbon at 6d; 4 laces of silk – 2 of one colour and 2 of another, price 8d [these were for lacing up doublets and gowns]; 3 dozen points, red and yellow, price 6d [to make it easier to thread the laces through the eyelets]; 3 pairs of pattens at about 2½d a pair but, I pray you, let them be long enough and broad upon the heel … [pattens were wooden-soled platform over-shoes to keep your feet raised above the mud so your shoes weren't spoiled].

Incidentally, one item of indispensable apparel for the housewife, rarely mentioned or illustrated, was the apron. Every wife would have worn one every day and its quality and colour would have indicated her social status. Forget the crisp, dazzling white starched affairs of Victorian maids. Medieval women wore aprons to keep their precious clothes clean; they would have been serviceable and wrap-around. The poor would have worn an apron of rough, hard-wearing frieze, probably in its natural undyed brownish colour. The better-off wives would have worn coloured aprons of linen, blue ones, dyed with woad, being a favourite Sunday going to church colour. For the wealthy, who had the time, an embroidered garment would be favoured, but could not be too elaborate as the garment would need to be washed frequently. Aprons were seen as *the* badge of respectability, so London's prostitutes were banned from wearing them!

The Goodman of Paris was quite particular about how his young wife should dress and behave in public:

> Know, dear sister, that if you wish to follow my advice you will have great care and regard for what you and I can afford to do, according to our estate. Have a care that you be honestly clad, without new devices and without too much or too little frippery [second-hand clothing]. And before you leave your chamber and house, take care first that the collar of your shift and of your blanchette, cotte and surcotte do not hang out, one over the other, as happens with certain drunken, foolish or witless women, who have no care for their honour, nor for the honesty of their estate or of their husbands, and who walk with roving eyes and head horribly reared up like a lion, their hair straggling out of their wimples, and the collars of their shifts and cottes crumpled, the one upon the other, and who walk mannishly and bear themselves uncouthly before folk without shame.

On the subject of behaviour, an anonymous verse, known as 'How the Good Wijf taughte hir Doughtir', has down-to-earth instructions for young women, to ensure that they will be more likely to capture a better husband if they behave suitably:

> When you sit in the church, your prayers you shall offer.
> Make you no chattering to friend or relation.
> Laugh you to scorn neither old folk nor young,
> But be of fair bearing and of good tongue.
> Through your fair bearing
> Your honour will increase,
> My dear child …
>
> Go you not into town as if you were a flighty person
> From one house to another in search of vain amusement;

And go not to market your burrel* to sell,
And then to the tavern to destroy your reputation.
For they that haunt taverns,
Their prosperity they bring down,
My dear child.

And if you be in a place where good ale is aloft,
Whether that you serve thereof, or that you sit quietly,
Moderately take you thereof that no blame befalls you,
For if you are often drunk, it reduces you to shame.
For those that be often drunk,
Prosperity is taken away from them,
My dear child.

Go not to wrestlings, nor to shooting at cock,
As if you were a strumpet or a wanton woman.
Stay at home daughter, and love your work much,
And so you shall, my dear child, soon grow rich.
It is evermore a merry thing,
A man to be served of his own thing,
My dear child.

Acquaint yourself not with each man that goes along the street;
If any man speak to you, swiftly you him greet.
Let him go by the way; do not stand by him,
That he by any villainy your heart might tempt.
For not all men are true
That know how to proffer fair words,
My dear child.

*burrel is cheap home-spun cloth

CHILDCARE

Until they were seven years old, children were thought to lack common sense and were in need of particularly close attention; it was part of the duties of the godparents, as promised at baptism, to keep their godchildren safe from fire and water. In an age of open fires and unguarded pots of boiling water, accidents could and did happen.

Children spent much of their first year swaddled in the cradle and, bearing in mind the cold, damp living conditions, swaddling might well have helped prevent chills. Swaddled babies were often hung from a peg on the wall, so they could see what was going on while keeping them safe and out of harm's way. The risk of having a baby crawl about on the floor by an unguarded fire or out of the door

Medieval mother and baby at the Loxwood Joust, 2014. (Glenn Mount)

into the street was too great. Cradle-fires were all too common as it seems cradles were often set too close to the fire. Evidence suggests babies were not swaddled all the time but allowed to crawl about, hopefully under supervision, in rooms, halls or gardens.

A baby's first few months were spent helpless with its mother as its primary carer, but life could still be hazardous. Matilda la Cambestere and her one-month-old daughter slept on the shop floor and although they were already asleep by curfew, Matilda had left a lighted candle on the wall. The candle fell onto the straw of the shop floor and they suffocated and were burned before the neighbours knew anything about it (Calendar for Coroners' Rolls of the City of London, 1337). Joan, also only a month old, the daughter of Bernard de Irlaunde, demonstrates another risk for children in London. Her parents lived in a rented shop in Queenhythe ward and an hour before vespers, her mother left her in her cradle with the shop door open since it was a pleasant May evening. While they were away, a pig came in and mortally bit the child's head. At length, her mother returned and snatched up Joan and kept her alive until midnight (Calendar for Coroners' Rolls, 1322). Pigs were strictly forbidden to be allowed to wander loose in the London streets, but they frequently did so.

For toddlers, life was even more fraught with danger. Three-year-old Petronilla de Wintonia was killed outside her father's house in August 1301 by a spirited horse, uncontrolled by its rider. Margery Lopechaunt wandered outside her parents' house in January 1339; it was so cold that she entered a neighbour's house where, going too close to the fire, she fell into a vessel of scalding water. That same year, seven-year-old John le Stolere, described as 'a pauper and beggar child', was crushed beneath a cart as he sat in the street to answer the call of nature.

Margery Hilton worked for a London baker and used to take her five-year-old with her. One of the baker's apprentices beat the child so severely that it died two

Woman with child in a walker. (MS 3384 Kongelige Bibliotek, Copenhagen)

Child rescued from the Thames at London Bridge. (MS Yates Thompson 47 f. 97, British Library – John Lydgate, Bury St Edmunds, 1461)

days later. What does become apparent from the statistics of child deaths is that boys tended to follow their fathers outside, suffering accidents with farm tools, falling out of trees or into ponds; girls tended to stay home with their mothers, suffering more burns and scalds, although there are cases also of outdoor activities, collecting water from the well being a time of hazard for small girls, all too liable to fall in.

Discipline was most important and it was believed that only corporal punishment could impress upon a child correct behaviour, moral judgement and proper respect for their elders. A five-year-old boy was in a neighbour's house when he took a piece of wool and put it in his cap. The lady of the house, chastising him, struck the boy with her right hand under his left ear. He cried out and his mother raised the hue and cry and carried him home where he died. The jury felt that his death was by misadventure – a necessary disciplinary action had unfortunately killed the boy. The neighbour was not indicted for murder. Eight-year-old Richard le Mazon was playing with his school friends, balancing along a beam that jutted from London Bridge out over the roiling waters of the Thames. Richard lost his footing and fell in, the weight of his school bag dragged him under and he drowned.

Bear in mind that these incidents, which seem to show that children must have perished at every turn, come from coroners' rolls. For the majority of children's mishaps, the outcome would not have been fatal – for every mortality there must have been dozens, perhaps hundreds of near misses, resulting in the usual scrapes and bruises experienced by all children every day. Sometimes they were fortunate enough to be rescued. However, the grim picture doesn't hide the fact that children were looked after and cared for, not only by their mothers but by godparents, family, servants, apprentices and neighbours. Everyone mourned those who died, but those who survived were loved, played with, trained and rewarded.

CHAUCER'S WIFE OF BATH
Perhaps the most famous medieval housewife is Chaucer's Wife of Bath.

> A good wif was ther of biside Bathe,
> But she was somdel deef, and that was scathe. [she was somewhat deaf, which was a pity]
> Of clooth-makyng she hadde swich an haunt [she had skill in cloth making]
> She passed hem of Ypres and of Gaunt. [she surpassed the cloth makers of Ypres and Ghent]
> In al the parisshe wif was ther noon
> That to the offrynge bifore hire sholde goon [proceeds];
> And if ther dide, certeyn so wrooth [angry] was she
> That she was out of all charitee. [she wouldn't forgive them]
> Hir coverchiefs [kerchief for the head] ful fyne weren of ground;
> I dorste swere they weyeden [weighed or cost] ten pound

That on a Sonday weren upon hir heed.
Hir hosen weren of fyn scarlet reed,
Ful streite yteyd [neatly tied], and shoos
ful moyste [supple] and newe.
Boold was hir face, and fair, and reed of
hewe.
She was a worthy womman al hir lyve:
Housbondes at chirche door she hadde
five …

This is part of Chaucer's description of the formidable, five-times-wed Wife of Bath in his prologue to the *Canterbury Tales*. In the prologue to her own tale, the wife tells us she is now eagerly awaiting husband number six. Although she was a virgin when first she wed, she doesn't see chastity as a virtue:

Wife of Bath, *Canterbury Tales*. (The Ellesmere Chaucer Huntington Library UC Berkeley EL26 C 9, London, 1410)

What good is a man if he only uses his sely instrument to urinate when he should use it for engendrure? Why else would God have made men and women as he did? Her next husband will be sette a-werke, she says, as the others were before him so that many a night they songen 'weilawey!'

CLEANLINESS

It is a common fallacy that medieval people were a dirty, smelly lot and, no doubt in the days before toilet soap and deodorants, sometimes that was the case (although alum stone, if wetted, applied like a roll-on deodorant and left to dry, works perfectly). As we have already heard, a husband expected to come home and have his feet bathed by his wife and clean socks afterwards. Considering the difficulty in preparing sufficient hot water for a bath, lugging it to and fro and warming the room so the bather should not catch their death, bathing did not happen too often but was popular, especially in summer (King John took a bath once a fortnight even in winter, as we know from his accounts: he usually paid his bath man 5*d* a day but 13*d* on bath nights!). John Russell gives instructions for preparing an upper-class husband's bath:

If your lord wishes to bathe and wash his body clean, hang sheets round the roof, every one full of flowers and sweet green herbs, and have five or six sponges to sit upon, and a sheet over so that he may bathe there for a while, and have a sponge also for under his feet, if there be any to spare, and always be careful that the door is shut. Have a basin full of hot fresh herbs and wash his body with a soft sponge, rinse him with fair rose water, and throw it over him; then let him go to bed; but see that the bed be sweet and nice; and first put on his socks and slippers that he may go near the fire and stand on his foot-sheet, wipe him dry with a clean cloth, and take him to bed to cure his troubles.

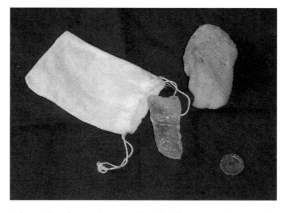

Alum 'deodorant' crystal and silk sponge 'tampon'. (Glenn Mount)

John Russell doesn't suggest that a wife should share her husband's bath but this was an enjoyable, popular and economic alternative in the great wooden tubs of the time. The sponges were necessary as cushions to guard against splinters. Incidentally, small 'silk' sponges were trimmed down and shaped for reusable tampons, being very soft and washable.

For the poorest folk, a quick dip in the river in warm weather was probably the best they could do. It was the later Tudors who decided bathing was all but suicidal, although Queen Elizabeth I did have a bath once a month 'whether she needed it or not'. Babies were bathed quite frequently, needing far less water anyway. A good housewife would grow her own supply of soapwort (*Saponaria*), the wetted leaves of which can be rubbed to give a smooth, creamy lather, gentle enough for faces and babies' bottoms, kinder than the homemade alkaline lye soap that was only suitable for doing the laundry.

We know medieval people were very particular about cleanliness at table too and it was good manners to wash your hands publicly both before, after and, if necessary, during the meal – after all, there were *no* forks.

PROVISIONS

The thickest chapter in the Goodman of Paris's book of instruction is concerned, not surprisingly, with food: growing it, shopping for it, preparation and presentation of it, all of which was either down to the housewife herself or, for the wealthy, down to her direction of the servants. Most houses, whether a peasant's hovel or a merchant's town house, had its own plot of ground on which to grow vegetables, herbs, fruit trees and, sometimes, to keep chickens, pigs, cows or other livestock. The garden was a larder, medicine chest, beautician's and perfumery all rolled into one.

The housewife would be skilled in the making of butter and cheese, using milk from the cow or the goats and sheep. Any dairy products and eggs surplus to household requirements could be sold at market and it was usually the housewife's prerogative to keep the profits, so it was worth her while to run the dairy efficiently.

> From April beginning till Andrew be past, [30 November]
> So long with good housewife her dairy doth last,
> Good milchcow and pasture, good husbands provide,
> The res'due good housewives know best how to guide.
>
> Ill housewife, unskilful to make her own cheese,
> Through trusting of others hath this for her fees:
> Her milk pan and cream pot so slabbered and sost
> That butter is wanting and cheese is half lost.

Brewing was also done at home and was a task not for the faint-hearted since it involved lugging and lifting large amounts of liquid, some of it boiling hot, keeping fires going all day and doors and window shutters open for good ventilation and cooling, no matter what the weather was like. However, the end product was worth it and it was infinitely preferable and safer than drinking possibly tainted water, but brewing was a long, strenuous task and, in medieval times, an almost exclusively female one.

So now we have butter, cheese, eggs and ale on the menu. From the garden we have cabbages (or 'caboches'), onions and leeks, carrots and turnips

A woman cooking at the Loxwood Joust, 2014. (Glenn Mount)

(strangely, often made into jam to preserve them), parsnips, which were considered a powerful aphrodisiac, and, when in season, fresh fruit. Out of season, fruits, flowers and even vegetables were turned into preserves or pickled, salted, dried or candied. For sweetening, there was honey – every village had its beekeeper and beehives, bees being vital to a good fruit harvest from the orchards. If you could afford it there was sugar, but this was always a luxury item, imported from Cyprus, Sicily or North Africa, yet medieval folk had such a sweet tooth that, given half a chance, the lady of the house would make candied rose petals, violets and marigolds, sugared nuts and confections of many kinds. She would also distil rosewater (a beauty product, perfume, medicine and cookery ingredient), lavender water, elderflower water, etc., and make homemade wines and cordials from anything available.

Dozens of herbs, edible and medicinal, were grown for home use, but the more exotic herbs and spices were imported from the Mediterranean and the East. This luxury trade could be very expensive, but some households could afford it. The Countess of Leicester, wife of Simon de Montfort, whose household accounts for Easter 1263 still survive, had a lavish shopping list:

> For 6lbs of ginger 15s. For 8lbs of pepper 18s. 8d. For 6lbs of cinnamon 6s. For 1lb of saffron 14s. For 12lbs of sugar [treated as a spice] 12s. For 6lbs of sugar with mace 6s. For one box of gingerbread 2s. 4d. For 10lbs of rice 15s. 3d. For 20lbs of almonds 4s. 2d.

Most of these ingredients would have been for cooking, but the housewife was also the family doctor. Sugar syrups with liquorice were considered the best treatment for chest complaints, if they could be afforded, and at least such a remedy must have tasted nice. Even if it didn't work, it wouldn't do the patient any harm, although it might eventually rot their teeth. Other medical recipes sound as though they might well have been quite effective, made from ingredients still used in pharmacy today.

> For the migraine – take half a dishful of barley, one handful each of betony, vervain and other herbs good for the head and when they be well boiled together, take them up and wrap them in a cloth and lay them to the sick head and it shall be whole.

Maggie Black, author of *The Medieval Cookbook*, has apparently tried this out successfully and today some of the chemicals obtained from betony are still used to treat nervous headaches and some kinds of migraine. Vervain derivatives are used to treat cases of migraine and depression so it seems the medieval housewife had got this treatment right. However, some medicines could never have worked and sound truly gruesome, like this fourteenth-century recipe from a fragment of the manuscript *Reliqiae Antiquae*:

> For him that has a quinsy – take a fat cat, and flay it well, and clean and draw out the guts, and take the grease of a hedgehog, and the fat of a bear, and resins and fenugreek, and sage, and gum of honeysuckle, and virgin wax; all this crumble small, and stuff the cat within as you stuff a goose; roast it all, and gather the grease and anoint him with it.

We must assume the more exotic ingredients were available from your local apothecary's shop.

Unless the house had its own stew pond, as some bigger houses did, the housewife would have to buy fish, whether fresh, dried or salted, from the market.

Apothecary's shop. (MS Sloane 1977 f. 49v, British Library – Mattheus Platearius, Amiens, France, first quarter of the fifteenth century)

Every household was obliged to eat fish on fast days, including every Wednesday, Friday and Saturday, throughout the forty days of Lent and the whole of Advent – no wonder the Countess of Leicester wanted to spice up her Easter dinner. Meat was also purchased at market, although those who kept pigs would have their own supply of bacon and hams. Ready-made meals could include sausages, black puddings and other cooked dishes like hot pigs' trotters and meat pies. There were vegetarian options too, such as 'hot peas-cods' – we would call them mange-touts. Although we tend to think of every housewife making her own scrumptious homemade bread, some houses could not afford the room or the fuel for a large baking oven, especially in crowded towns – London actually legislated against houses having large ovens. There were two alternatives in this case: either the housewife could make her own bread dough and pies and take them to the baker to be cooked, or she could buy them hot from the baker or street vendor – 'take-away' is not a twentieth-century invention.

COOKING AND SERVING MEALS

When it came to cooking meat, fish and vegetables at home, the housewife required the right equipment and, again, Ellen Langwith's will provides us with an insight as to what was needed:

> 2 quart pots, 2 pint pots, all of pewter, 3 brass pots of various sizes, a pair of racks [as for barbequing], 2 new brass pans, another brass pan, 2 laten chafer dishes, a little chafer dish with 2 ears, 2 iron spits (1 long, 1 short), 2 chargers and a pewter garnish vessel.

Bread oven at the
Weald and Downland
Open Air Museum.
(Glenn Mount)

All this went to John Brown, of course.

Pottages, thick soups almost like our porridge (from which the word is derived), were a popular starter for an elaborate meal, or, for the poorer household, the main course. Here is the Goodman of Paris's detailed recipe for a winter pottage:

> Peel onions and boil them in slices, then fry them in a pot. Now behoveth it to have your chicken cleft across the back and grilled on the grill over a coal fire, or if it be veal the same; and let the veal be put in in gobbets and the chicken in quarters and put them with the onions in the pot; then have white bread toasted on the grill and steeped in the sewe of another meat; and then bray ginger, clove, grain of paradise and long pepper, moisten them with verjuice and wine (but strain them not) and set them aside. Then bray the bread and run it through a strainer and put it in the brewet and let all strain together and boil; then serve it forth.

The 'sewe' of another meat means the juices, 'grain of paradise' is a kind of pepper, 'verjuice' is crab-apple juice – very sharp indeed – and a 'brewet' was a cooking pot.

Having cooked the meal, it then had to be served correctly whether a feast or an informal supper for one. Hands would be washed as the diners came in or were seated at the table. The table had to be correctly laid with table cloths, napkins and a salt cellar. Diners brought their own knives, but forks did not appear at table, although spiky implements were used in the kitchen for handling hot meats. Spoons were provided: wooden for the poor, pewter, then silver for the better off. Ellen Langwith left twelve silver spoons in her will (to John Brown), described as having 'spear-points' so might have been double-ended precursors to the table fork and used to spear sticky sweetmeats. She also left three silver masers, which were wide drinking cups on pedestals, usually two handled and often with lids that would have been shared by diners, according to their rank. Ellen bequeathed a little cup with silver and gilt roses round the foot to her friend Ellen Warren, wife of a London fuller. Many of these valuable items of tableware may never have been used, unless perhaps royalty called, but would have been displayed on an elegant buffet or cupboard (dresser) to impress visitors.

The meal itself would have seemed odd to us because medieval folk loved to mix sweet and savoury: apple sauce with pork and honey-glazed ham are the modern vestiges of this tradition. Pungent sauces were served at every opportunity, with lots of vinegar, verjuice and wine, if the household could afford it, used in the cooking, and sweet spices, like cinnamon and cloves, were served with meat and fish. Pottages could be sweet or savoury, as could blancmange which might have such things as chopped veal and raisins added to it. Rice was more commonly used than you might think and was, like blancmange, often mixed with meat and fruit and, having been boiled in a cloth, would be served cold, set by the meat juices and sliced.

Between courses, 'dainties' or 'subtleties' would be served. This might mean a dish of sugared almonds for a humble meal or a confectioner's work of art

Women in the kitchen. (*Tacuinum Sanitatis*, Vienna)

Busy housewives at the Loxwood Joust, West Sussex, 2014. (Glenn Mount)

Above left: A woman weaving with la lucette at the Loxwood Joust, West Sussex, 2014. (Glenn Mount)

made of icing and 'marchpane', like that of a man on horseback, stealing a tiger's cubs – a fantastic construction produced for the marriage feast of Henry V and Katherine de Valois in 1420. Of course, such a wonder was not usually within the scope of the average housewife as the cost of sugar alone would be prohibitive, but a simpler creation, like miniature marzipan fruits, might well be possible for a feast day dinner.

When the meal was over, the washing up had to be done; cooking pots and wooden trenchers required scouring with sand and washing in water as hot as possible. This was all very hard on the hands, although a homemade salve of goose grease, sage and marigolds might help when the work was done. However, as Thomas Tusser tells us, 'Some respite to husbands the weather may send; / But housewives' affairs have never an end'.

Left: The interior of Hangleton cottage, at the Weald and Downland Museum, Sussex. This would have been a poor person's house. (Glenn Mount)

Below: The interior of Bayleaf house at the Weald and Downland Museum – the house of a well-to-do person – showing the pantry and buttery off the screens passage. (Glenn Mount)

A fifteenth-century street scene at the Weald and Downland Museum, with a shop on the left with jettied upper storeys, which would have been common in medieval towns. (Glenn Mount)

A shop entrance, showing the outside counter (showing board). (Glenn Mount)

3

Women in Trade

Before the Industrial Revolution and the invention of large-scale factories, towns were the centres of trade where manufacturing went on in small domestic workshops. Sales tended to be direct from the producer to the customer, in the case of crafts at the small business end of the market. Items like saddles and horse harness, books and pots all came direct from the saddler, lorimer, stationer and potter and might well be made to order. But the quantities dealt with in these cases would have been beneath the attention of the prosperous merchants. They were more interested in wholesale imports and exports of wool, cloth, spices and wines. So where did women fit into these various commercial ventures?

Women at a market stall at the Battle of Tewkesbury re-enactment, 2014. (Pat Patrick)

In training young girls for their future roles in life, the intention was to make them useful, with a sense of economic responsibility and, at the same time, to keep them amenable to male authority. The relative emphasis put on each of these three virtues: usefulness, thrift and subservience to men, varied with the wealth and inclinations of the girls' parents. Wealthy, landed merchants might look forward to marrying their daughters into the gentry and engage a governess to look after the girls and instruct them, French and needlework being preferred subjects. However, it was not uncommon to apprentice girls to learn a trade, so they might be self-supporting, if need be, or of assistance to their future husbands. Pecock, in his writings *The Reule of Cristen Religioun*, said that it was a wife's duty, if her husband wished it, to use her spare time in contributing to the support of the household and, certainly among the poorer classes in the City of London, this was the custom. There were women householders among all classes and 4 per cent of London taxpayers in 1319 were women; some were wealthy *rentiers* (landlords), but most were identified in the list simply by their name and their trade:

> Elena la juelera, paying 8*d*. Matilla la bracereste, 10*d*. Petronilla la brewere, 12*d*. Margeria la sylkewymman, 13*d*. Alic la stocfysshmonger, 14*d*. A coifer, a leach and a saddler, each 20*d*. A spurrier and a girdler, each 3*s*. 4*d*. Dyonisia la bokebyndere, 6*s*. 8*d*.

In the wealthier merchant households, the wife's business ventures weren't always an economic necessity, but would earn them some extra spending money, or 'pin-money'. Yet there were times when a wife might have a vital role to play in overseeing her husband's affairs in his absence, perhaps while he was working abroad. Margery Kempe (born *c*.1373) was the wife of one of the wealthiest merchants at Lynn (Kings Lynn, Norfolk), but she took up brewing and then the grinding of corn in a horse mill because she did not want any other woman in the town to be 'arrayed so well as she'. In London, a fishmonger's heiress, who was married four times, continued both brewing and tailoring. A fishmonger's widow bequeathed a male apprentice all the anvils and equipment from some kind of metal-working shop that had been in her charge. Dame Elizabeth Stokton ran a business of cloth manufacture for export to Italy, but the more usual trades taken up by women were embroidery, the 'garnishing' of clothing with jewels or other decoration and the manufacture of silk. This last process was managed almost entirely by merchants' wives, some of them having the raw silk imported by their husbands.

ALICE CLAVER, A FIFTEENTH-CENTURY SILKWOMAN

Some women, particularly in the fourteenth and fifteenth centuries, were running businesses in their own right – these women were legally termed *femmes soles*.

One such woman who made a success of her independent career was Alice Claver. Alice, the second wife of Richard Claver, a wealthy London mercer, having completed her apprenticeship, was left a widow with a baby son in 1456. Her husband's will states that she had been working as a silkwoman, *femme sole*, during his lifetime. After his death, Alice continued her work, occasionally being employed by the king's Great Wardrobe. She made tassels for Edward IV's books, silk ribbons to lace points and to make girdles (belts), buttons of blue and gold silk, fringing of Venice gold at 6*s* an ounce, coloured fringing and an elaborate garter, perhaps an 'Order of the Garter' insignia rather than a garter to hold up a stocking since a single item was ordered. She also provided four counterpanes with embroidered images and scriptural text in various colours, trimmed with the Yorkist badges of suns, crowns and roses. In July 1483 Alice supplied the great lace mantle and the silk tassels for the king's gloves for the coronation of Richard III and Queen Anne. She never remarried and, at her death in 1489, Alice left her business to her apprentice, Katherine Champyon.

The statutes of the City of London for the 1450s tell us that the manufacture of silk was specifically a woman's business, unlike embroidery, hosiery or even laundering. The statutes state:

> Many a worshipful woman within the city has lived full honourably and therewith many good households kept, and many gentlewomen and others, more than a thousand, have been apprenticed under them in learning the same craft of silk making.

The craft of silk-working was extremely skilled. Some London silkwomen ran extensive workshops and took on apprentices from as far away as Yorkshire. To buy the raw materials and offer credit to customers, they would have needed plenty of capital and often cooperated among themselves to raise the cash. When a girl completed her apprenticeship, she didn't join a guild, as a man would do, but remained with her mistress until she married and was able to set up a shop for herself. Alice Claver relied on the support and friendship of other silkwomen, especially Beatrice Fyler who seems to have been close to Alice. In the 1480s Alice also had a widow, Katherine Hardman, come to live with her. The silkwomen took on each other's daughters as apprentices (Katherine Champyon was one), witnessed each other's wills, acted as executors and stood sureties for each other – all offices usually undertaken by fellow guild members. In the late fourteenth century, when the silkwomen's businesses were threatened by foreign competition, they banded together and successfully petitioned Parliament and the Lord Mayor for support, but they never achieved guild status. Unfortunately, this lack of a proper guild was the downfall of the craft as a women-only monopoly. When men moved into the silk-working industry in the sixteenth century due to rising unemployment, the silkwomen could do nothing to prevent them from taking over.

HELPING THE 'OTHER HALF'

Married women in towns all over England frequently helped their husbands in their businesses or shops and were usually responsible for selling the finished product. If a man was a weaver, his wife might operate one of the looms. The wives of tailors, cordwainers (shoemakers) and glovers did much of the sewing involved in the manufacture of the goods. Even when men carried out a trade such as building construction or casting bronze or pewter, crafts that did not readily allow female involvement, wives could still learn about accounting and be responsible for paying wages and hiring workers.

Christine de Pisan, in her book, *The Treasure of the City of Ladies*, instructs:

> All wives of artisans should be very painstaking and diligent if they wish to have the necessities of life. They should encourage their husbands or their workmen to get to work early in the morning and work until late, for mark our words, there is no trade so good that if you neglect your work you will not have difficulty putting bread on the table. And besides encouraging the others, the wife herself should be involved in the work to the extent that she knows all about it, so that she may know how to oversee his workers if her husband is absent, and to reprove them if they do not do well. She ought to oversee them from idleness, for through careless workers the master is sometimes ruined. And when customers come to her husband and try to drive a hard bargain, she ought to warn him solicitously to take care that he does not make a bad deal. She should advise him to be chary of giving too much credit if he does not know where and to whom it is going, for in this way many come to poverty, although sometimes the greed to earn more or to accept a tempting proposition makes them do it.

Woman stitching a purse from the Free Company at the Loxwood Joust, West Sussex, 2014. (Glenn Mount)

The fact that craftsmen's wives were a crucial part of the skilled workforce shows up clearly in ordinances, such as that of the York Founders' Guild, who allowed members who did not have wives to take on one more apprentice than was normally permitted, to make up for the lack. Also, legislation forbidding the employment of women (usually in times of unemployment for men) almost always exempted wives and sometimes daughters too. By far the most common kind of work for women was serving in the shop, looking after customers while the husband worked elsewhere, but there are a few cases of women doing very responsible jobs. Alice was married to Nicholas Holford, the bailiff of London Bridge. His task was to work out the fee due for every cart, dray or flock of sheep or geese which crossed the bridge, according to the goods being carried, the number of animals and the people involved, whether owning or simply transporting or herding the merchandise. When Nicholas died in 1433, Alice took over the complicated task and proved so efficient – and, presumably, good at arithmetic – that she remained at her post for a further twenty years.

As we've already seen, some married women carried out a trade separate from their husbands', though, quite often, the two trades were connected – like the silkwomen relying on raw materials imported by their husbands. A wife married to a butcher might make tallow candles and black puddings. In Coventry, knitting involved a large number of women working from home and, all over the country, wives supplemented the family income by carding and spinning wool. The small-metal trades of goldsmithing and pin and nail manufacture also employed married and single women on a piece work basis.

A few women were employed as midwives and sick-nurses and everywhere, whether married or not, women worked as laundresses; however, as revealed by King Edward IV's Wardrobe Accounts, men did laundry too. In Westminster, the wife of Robert Harrison, a smith, worked on her own account, washing and mending clothes, including vestments for the parish church of St Margaret's, but we know very little of this trade. Questions remain, such as whether the women washed the clothes or the linen in the home of their employers or whether the dirty washing was brought to the laundress's own house. The wages were often dismal, such as the 4*d* a week that was paid to the wife of John Hayn for washing the linen of the entire household of Sir Henry Stafford. The money may have provided a little useful extra income but it certainly wasn't enough to live on. Doing laundry was never a well paid job: the Bishop of Coventry's household accounts for 1461 show that Joan Boteler of Heywood was paid just 2*s* for washing three dozen linen cloths from the lord bishop's chamber and nine dozen from his pantry and scullery. The churchwardens of St Ewen's, in Bristol, paid William Clerk's wife only 16*d* for washing the church vestments and ornaments for a whole year. St Mary at Hill church

Washerwomen. (Splendor Solis, Nuremberg, 1531)

in London paid a little better as Alice Smale earned 3*s* 4*d* for washing the church linen for a year. Perhaps the worst paid was Hugh Praune's wife as she was paid the miserly sum of 4*d* for making 140 lbs of Paris candles – a whole year's work – by Robert Waterton in 1417.

Where wages were concerned, even the silkwomen could never earn as much as their husbands. A few women working as independent brewers may have produced a reasonable income, but women in this trade tended to come from better-off families anyway – one reason for this may have been that the initial outlay for brewing equipment was quite costly. The job needed large vats, pans and barrels and plenty of fuel for the fires which had to be kept burning for the brewing process. However, a large proportion of the working female population was made up of hucksters and spinsters, women who worked long hours for low profits. As these women didn't earn sufficient income to become *femmes soles*, their husbands, as head of the household, controlled all the family finances, including his wife's, however meagre her wages. The women also had to do the extra work in addition to their regular domestic chores. Records show that few spinsters, hucksters and even embroiderers could afford servants and men were most unlikely to share the tasks of laundry or childcare, so the extra money was probably earned at the cost of utter exhaustion.

THE WILL OF DAME ELIZABETH COOK

Women didn't leave wills very often. Only on rare occasions did a wife write a will and then it had to be with her husband's consent. Most of the women who did leave wills were the widows of wealthy merchants or even merchants in their own right. Elizabeth Cook (or Coke as the scribe has spelt it) was the widow of Sir Thomas Cook, a wealthy merchant and Lord Mayor of London in 1462–63. He was a draper by trade and had succeeded in persuading King Edward IV to grant the Drapers' Company Charter in 1481.

The Cook family's secretary, John Vale (or John Devale, as he is referred to in Dame Elizabeth's will), left extensive records of his master's and mistress's affairs so

A woman archer at England's Medieval Festival, Herstmonceux, 2014. (Pat Patrick)

we know that Thomas Cook, although a Yorkist supporter in the main, married Elizabeth Malpas, daughter and co-heiress of Alderman Philip Malpas, a fellow draper but ardent supporter of the House of Lancaster. They were wed in the early years of the Wars of the Roses and their first child, Philip, was born in 1454. There were three other sons also: Thomas, who died young; John, who is mentioned in Elizabeth's will; and the youngest, William, who was still a child when their mother died. There was also a daughter, Joan or Joanna, who was wed to John Forster – both mentioned in the will.

In her will, Elizabeth is bequeathing her own inheritance, i.e. properties she had inherited from her father, Philip Malpas, leaving all to her son John, daughter Joanna and secretary John Devale, none of whom had gained much from Thomas Cook's will in 1478. The main beneficiary of Thomas's will had been the eldest son, Philip, who was proving himself a dissolute wastrel and not a good candidate for the inheritance of precious estates. As long ago as 1469, when he was only fifteen, Grandfather Malpas had described his grandson and namesake as 'lacking good rule', so Elizabeth's will overrides her husband's in respect of properties inherited from the Malpas side of the family. Unfortunately, John Cook died soon after his mother and the youngest, William, with help from the secretary, John Devale and brother-in-law, John Forster, spent years fighting through the courts to gain his share of the family estates which had been seized by his elder brother Philip, who had run up sizeable debts by this time.

Of particular interest is Elizabeth's bequest to John Devale of her two shops in Bridge Street, London, which suggests she was running a business in her own right. Unfortunately, her will says nothing of what was sold in her shops, but other sources give John Devale both as a dealer in the book trade and a draper. Whether these references might shed light on the trade carried out in Elizabeth Cook's shops, we don't know for certain.

However, there were a few cases of women making wills in their own right even when their husbands were still alive. Emma, the wife of Henry de Preston, at one time Lord Mayor of York, got Henry's consent to make her will in 1401 and made him her executor. She left 100s each to her son and daughter, 20s to her sister-in-law and 5 marks to Alice Stede to assist her in marriage, though Alice had to behave herself, remain a virgin and of good repute until she found a husband in order to be entitled to the whole sum. For the rest, Emma was only able to distribute her clothes and to give some of her own jewels and ornamented girdles to her daughter. Another case involves Isobel Dove in 1435. Her husband was overseas when she wrote her will, so she named a female friend as her executrix. This friend was given the guardianship of Isobel's goods with the duty of settling her debts (suggesting Isobel was a *femme sole*), paying for her burial and carrying out her bequests. The executrix was then to keep the remainder of the goods until Isobel's husband came home.

FEMMES SOLES AND FEMMES COUVERTES

In 1364, sureties were taken for Agnes, the wife of a London cutler, that she would teach Jusema, her apprentice, and feed and clothe her and not beat her with a stick or knife. In 1376, also in London, William and Johanna Kaly petitioned the court that their apprentice, Alice Cook, might take a husband if she liked and could still continue her apprenticeship if she wished, or be released upon payment of 4 marks, as she preferred. It was more usual for apprentices to have taken a solemn oath not to get married, frequent taverns, nor tell their master's secrets nor rob him of more than 6*d* a year.

Women apprenticed in this way could support themselves by their craft if they remained unmarried and were designated *femmes soles*. However, we know many married women went on with their own jobs after marriage, carrying on a trade quite separate from their husbands'. Regulations of many medieval towns provided for the treatment of a wife as a single woman in such cases. If she became involved in a trade dispute, she was not 'covered' by her husband, which meant that he wasn't responsible for her debts as he would otherwise be. For example, the rules of the city of Lincoln state,

> If any woman that has a husband use any craft within the city, whereof her husband meddles not, she shall be charged as a sole woman as touching such things as belongeth to her craft. And if a plaint be taken against such a woman, she shall answer and plead as a sole woman and make her law and take other advantage in court by plea or otherwise for her discharge. And if she be condemned she shall be committed to prison till she be agreed with the plaintiff, and no goods or chattels that belongeth to the husband shall be confiscated.

We find similar rules in London and many other towns. They were intended for the protection of husbands but, nonetheless, represented an advance in the position of married women under the common law. Medieval industry was open to women and they played a considerable part in it. There were few crafts in which women are not found. According to records throughout England, women worked as butchers, chandlers, ironmongers, net makers, shoemakers, glovers, girdlers, haberdashers, purse makers, cap makers, skinners, bookbinders, gilders, painters, spicers, smiths and goldsmiths, these trades being just a sample. The involvement of women in so many trades was sometimes a cause for concern. Their wages were lower than men's, even for the same work, and men were afraid of being undercut by cheap labour.

At Bristol in 1461, the complaint was made that weavers were hiring women other than their wives and daughters:

> by the which many & divers of the King's liege people, likely men to do the king service in his wars and defence of this land and sufficiently learned in the said craft goeth vagrant and unoccupied and may not have their labour to their living.

The Moneylender and His Wife, by Quentin Matsys. 1456. (The Yorck Project 10000 Meisterwerke der Malerei, Netherlands, first half of the sixteenth century)

The position here was similar to that after the two world wars in that, while the men were away fighting, women had taken over their jobs. Then, when the men returned, employers were not so keen to give them their old jobs back, having discovered women just as efficient but requiring lower wages. The result was the unemployment of healthy males, a situation the guilds set out to remedy as occasion demanded. The Lincoln Fullers passed rules preventing women, apart from wives and daughters of masters, working at the trade in 1297, after a series of active campaigns in Scotland; the London Girdlers did the same in 1344 during a lull in the Hundred Years War.

What rights did women have in the medieval craft guilds? Certainly, women were members of social and religious guilds, which were commonly associated with particular crafts and, as wives and daughters, they took part in the social and religious activities connected with those guilds. Yet there was the possibility, in a few cases, of women becoming guild members in their own right, explicitly mentioned as members among the male masters. For example, women became members of the Guild of the Barber-Surgeons of York and London and the Dyers Guild of Bristol, but the majority of these were probably widows of past members. By the London custom, widows of London freemen were themselves recognised as freewomen of the city, able to continue their husbands' trades as members of the craft guilds as if they were members. London records contain plenty of references to male apprentices who, on the death of their master, continued to serve with their widows.

One example is William Caxton, famous for introducing printing to England, who was apprenticed as a young man to Robert Large, a London mercer. Robert Large died in 1441, leaving his wife Johanna to continue the business and the training of his five apprentices, including William, each receiving 20 marks in their master's will. Johanna kept her husband's mercery business running at least until her marriage to John Gedney three years later, by which time William had completed his apprenticeship and was plying his trade in the Low Countries.

As a widow, according to London custom, Johanna's freewoman status would have allowed her to conduct business in the city, take on apprentices (both male and female), open a shop and trade retail, 'wage her law in the city courts' – that is clear herself of charges by producing a specified number of oath-helpers in case of prosecution – and if she traded outside the city, her goods would be privileged in other towns and markets like those of other London citizens. However, had Johanna Large been a widow in Exeter, she would have no comparable privileges. In York, she might have been able to purchase similar rights, depending on the guild to which her husband had belonged. Elsewhere, as in Canterbury, Hull, Nottingham and Shrewsbury, women had to buy a licence to trade, whatever their marital status.

The alternative designation for a married woman was a *femme couverte*, literally 'covered' in law by her husband. She could still run a business of her own and take on apprentices, but all contracts and indentures had to be sealed by her husband, and any profits were legally his, as were any debts or fines to be paid for malpractice accrued by his wife. The majority of working wives were *femmes couvertes* and so legally 'invisible', their husbands being responsible under the law. The London borough ordinances of 1419 state that

> married women who follow certain crafts in the city by themselves without their husbands may take women as their apprentices to serve them and to learn their crafts, and these apprentices shall be bound by their indentures of apprenticeship to the husband and his wife to learn the wife's craft.

A busy housewife takes a few moments to rest at the Loxwood Joust, West Sussex, 2014. (Glenn Mount)

REGRATORS, FORESTALLERS AND HUCKSTERS

The Borough Ordinances for York in 1301 describe regrators as unworthy souls, since this was an occupation often carried out by women who were less than scrupulous. Not surprisingly, they appeared before the Boards of Assizes quite frequently, a fact which probably makes the number of women employed in regrating seem relatively high compared with other kinds of employment.

> Concerning regrators who buy badly-baked bread, and short-weight bread, and mix good and bad together, thus selling bread and ale contrary to the assize, it is ordered that no regrator shall sell any merchandise for more than the tradesman who produced it. Anyone so convicted shall be punished exactly like the tradesman. Regrators shall not place bread together with oil, butter, fat and other contaminating goods in their windows for sale, as they used to do, but bread shall be placed by itself, cheese by itself, and all kinds of goods separately, so they do not affect each other, but are properly, honestly and individually set out for sale. If butter and fat are found together in a regrator's window for sale, they shall be forfeit, and the finder shall have them, by view of the bailiffs of the city or any of those appointed to keep these ordinances.

The York assizes lists eighteen women prosecuted as regrators but only eight men and, unfortunately, the dishonesty of regrators was virtually a tradition, as was the common practice of regrators dabbling in a variety of trades all at once, making them seem greedy for business of any kind. So we are not surprised when, in *Piers Plowman*, written by William Langland in the second half of the fourteenth century, we meet Rose the regrator, the wife of Avarice:

> My wife was a weaver and woollen cloth made
> She spake to the spinners to spinnen it out.
> … I bought her barley malt, she brew it to sell.
> … Rose the regrator was her right name
> She hath holden huckstery all her life time.

In other words, Rose carried on trading as a weaver and brewer and also as a huckster or retailer of food and drink.

Forestallers were even more unpopular, as self-appointed middlemen, driving up market prices. The York civic ordinances state that

> It is ordained that no forestaller shall go out of the city by land or water to buy meat, fish or other merchandise being brought to the city, nor shall anyone sell the merchandise of others. Anyone convicted is to go to the pillory, from the hour of prime to midday for the first offence. For the second, they are to be dragged on a hurdle from the church of St Michael at the bridge over the Ouse, through the middle of the main street to the great church of St Peter. For the

third offence, they shall be imprisoned for forty days, and then be exiled from the city.

The Lincoln peace sessions for 1375 includes

Item. They present that Agnes, wife to William Sadelere of Louth is a common forestaller of both salt and fresh fish at Louth and elsewhere in this year ... by meeting fish before it could come to market and, having bought it by forestalling, sold it retail and made an excessive profit of 10s against the form of the ordinance ...

The Leet Court at Norwich in 1288 makes forestalling sound an even more underhanded crime:

They also say that Millicent de Melton, the wife of Henry the carpenter of Sucling, secretly buys grain before it comes to market, and she is accustomed so to do.

A huckster was a women ('huckster' is a feminine noun) who sold food and drink, not from a proper shop or market stall, but would take a barrow or carry a tray of wares around the streets. Such women were frequently in trouble for their unofficial trading which they usually did without a licence. One reason for this was that only citizens or wives or widows of citizens could get a licence to trade, so many women had no alternative if they were to make a living at all. Some could be quite enterprising, like the brewsters of St Ives at the Bishop of Ely's court, concerning the local fair in 1300:

The brewsters selling ale in boats and carrying measures into court ... Agnes Hervy of Ely, having a boat, brought a gallon, a pottle, and a quart. The quart was sealed and was found false. It was broken by judgement in full court.

WOMEN OF THE NIGHT
The oldest profession known to mankind, prostitution, was as common during the medieval period as at any other time in our history. What was the attitude, during this period, to a 'business' that has always been considered disreputable but necessary? Christine de Pisan gives us a clue to the opinion of a respectable Parisian lady in her very first paragraph on the subject from her book, *The Treasure of the City of Ladies*:

Just as the sun shines on the just and the unjust, we have no shame in extending our instruction even to the women who are foolish and loose and lead disorderly lives, although there is nothing more abominable. Nor should we feel any shame, recalling that Jesus Christ Himself felt no repugnance in showing such women

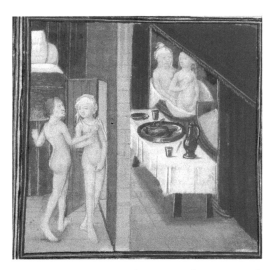

Prostitutes. (MS Royal 17 F IV f.297, British
Library – Luxury, *Le livre de Valerius Maximus*,
France, third quarter of the fifteenth century)

the error of their ways and turning them away from sin. Therefore, for charity and goodness and so that some of them may perhaps retain from our teachings something that may rescue them from their disreputable lives, we will teach them something. A greater act of charity cannot be performed than to rescue a sinner from evil and from sin.

In Roman times, prostitution was seen as a necessary evil. Medieval Christian lawyers inherited this attitude and set up numerous restrictions affecting prostitutes. These women could not accuse others of crimes, were forbidden to inherit property and had to use a representative to answer any charges made against them in a court of law. It was only in the later Middle Ages that the moral outrage against such women finally relented and allowed them to keep any money made from their illicit trade, although it was suggested such earnings should be given to the Church as alms for the poor and needy.

From the middle of the thirteenth century, London issued and reissued a series of regulations insisting that all prostitutes should be housed either in Cock Lane in Smithfield or in the much larger Southwark stews across the Thames on Bankside. At the time, Southwark belonged to the Bishop of Winchester. It was his London estate and he had a valuable collection of liberties and privileges in the borough. The supervision of the Southwark stews and the collection of the profits made by any of the Bishop of Winchester's 'geese' were in the hands of his staff. By the fifteenth century, the bishop's estate controlled the rent, organised weekly inspections of the prostitutes' quarters and ordered that enquiries should be made into the money owed by each individual, including the stew-holders, the prostitutes and the officials carrying out the inspection. The Bishop's documents also set out the fines for breaking the rules.

Almost all regulations concerning prostitutes insisted on their wearing a special mark on their clothing and tried to forbid them from flaunting jewels, furs and silks, as well as confining them to a particular area of town. London was kinder than some European cities – Paris forbade shoulder capes, coral rosaries and books of hours with a silver clasp. London was content, in 1351, to insist only that prostitutes should not 'be clad in manner and dress of good and noble dames and damsels of the realm in unreasonable manner', but they should wear an unlined hood of striped cloth. Other regulations tried to limit working hours and deal with sanitary precautions. The Southwark customs declared that prostitutes should work minimal hours on feast days and not at the time of church services. The women were not to work at night during sessions of Parliament (so as not to draw MPs away from more important business) and would be fined 6s 8d every night they did so. Stewholders (brothel-keepers) were forbidden from keeping single women against their will, from accepting married women, nuns or those who were pregnant or had the 'burning sickness' (venereal disease). The women must not be charged more than 14d a week for their chamber, nor forced to eat at the stew, nor could they sell any food or drink. The women must not drag a man in by his hood or gown, but should let him choose freely whether to enter or not, nor could they take his money and then refuse to lie with him. They were not allowed to have a lover of their own or to wear an apron – which, as we've seen, was a mark of respectability. Only a man or a husband and wife could run a stew, which was, in theory, just a bath-house where you could 'stew' in hot water, but everyone knew what other pleasures were available too. If a single woman or widow kept her own establishment, she broke the custom of the manor and was to be fined 20s at every court until the matter was resolved – perhaps by her marriage.

In 1483, in York, the borough records note:

> Cherrylips. Memorandum that 12th day of May ... the whole parish of St Martin in Micklegate came before my lord the mayor and complained of Margery Grey, otherwise called Cherrylips, that she was a woman ill disposed of her body to whom ill disposed men resort to the annoyance of her neighbours.

Clearly, not all prostitutes conducted their trade under supervision and in designated areas and, sadly, some weren't permitted even to continue their trade in safety. The coroner's court in London in 1301 recorded the death of Christine de Menstre in the churchyard of St Mary Woolchurch:

> ... She lay dead of death other than her rightful death ... three good men of the ward say on their oath that the preceding Sunday evening a certain William le Sawiere met the said Christina in the churchyard and asked her to spend the night with him and she refused and endeavoured to escape from his hands. The said William, moved with anger, drew a certain Irish knife and struck the said Christina under the right shoulder blade, causing a wound an inch broad and six inches deep, of which wound she then and there died ...

FEMININE TRADERS' SURNAMES
Here is a selection of surnames derived from women's trades:

Throwster: female silk weaver.
Huckster: female pedlar or hawker of food or drink.

Brewster: female brewer.
Tapster: female seller of ale.
Spinster: female spinner of wool or flax.
Baxter: female baker.
Tranter: female street trader, like a huckster.
Kempster: female who cards and combs wool ready for spinning.

From the Bishop of Ely's fair court at St Ives in 1302:

From Margaret de Rydon, Baxter, for a wastel-bread of Alice de Northampton, regratress, deficient in weight forty pence and for default of thirty pence in weight in a wastel-bread of Alice de Fenton, regratress, *6d.*

More unusual feminine surnames come from trades you might not usually associate with women:

Thaxter: female thatcher.
Pallister: female who constructs paling fences.
Hewster: female hewer of wood.
Beggister: female beggar.
Dyster: female dyer.
Whister: female whiter, a bleacher of linen.
Corvester: female cordwainer or shoemaker.

Billingsters (agricultural workers) and Filisters (who may have been involved in carpentry) are also mentioned, but their roles remain unclear. There even existed bellringsters, hoardsters and washsters! All of them were twelfth- and thirteenth-century words. Also recorded is Matilda la Barbaresse who had apprentices.

5

Peasant Women

Despite the fact that during the medieval period the majority of the population of England could have been described as 'peasants', this class of people, being taken so much for granted, is the least prominent class in the contemporary sources. Usually, when peasants are referred to, it is the men rather than the women who get mentioned. Therefore, the largest class of working women, living and labouring on manor lands throughout the country, seldom appear in literature of any kind, poverty being deemed neither romantic nor inspiring. In order to discover something of the lives and loves of these unsung heroines, we have to cast the net wider than usual, sometimes for little result, but with the occasional gem turning up to surprise us.

A housewife at the Loxwood Joust, West Sussex, 2014. (Glenn Mount)

Even among the peasantry there were subclasses based on social standing, economic and legal status. The lowest class could be divided roughly into two groups, 'ploughmen' and 'labourers'. Ploughmen were relatively self-sufficient farmers, tilling their own lands, while labourers earned wages, usually by working someone else's land. Ploughmen might be reasonably well off and hold many plots of manor land. At the opposite end of the scale were the poorest labourers, paid by the day and known as 'cottars' because the hut or cottage was usually all they had and they struggled desperately to grow enough food on the village commons to feed themselves and their families.

Another important factor was whether the ploughman or labourer was free or unfree. In the later Middle Ages, the possibility of buying your freedom changed some of these class divisions. In England, tenants (or bondsmen and bondswomen) who held land from their lord and were forbidden to leave the manor except in certain rare cases, were known as 'villeins'. They were unfree but had particular rights. In Europe, bondsmen were 'serfs' and had fewer rights and less freedom than their English fellows. Bondsmen and women usually owed their lord more rents and services than did their free neighbours and had little chance to better themselves. They weren't allowed to become members of the clergy or to take their legal cases to a royal court if they disagreed with their lord's idea of justice.

Two cases show how different the situation could be for women, although both were officially 'peasants'. In 1377, Agnes, daughter of Thomas atte Lowe, took up a holding in Moor that had been given up by a former tenant. It consisted of a messuage, which was a house plot with its small courtyard and a virgate of land, probably around fifteen acres. She would be responsible for the rates and services due and hold it according to the custom of the manor. However, Agnes was still a child so her father would make sure the rents were paid and the services carried out until she came of age. He also guaranteed to build a house on the messuage. All this made little Agnes a very desirable bride. Once married, her husband would take over her father's responsibility and become the official tenant, although Agnes might be able to ensure that this holding, having been specifically given to her by her father, would pass to her preferred choice of heir after her husband's death and her own. At the other end of the village social scale, Alice de Schishurst of Halesowen is a sad example of the poor peasant woman and her marginal situation. Both Alice's brother and nephew were servants for richer peasants (perhaps like Agnes's family above), but since she found no employment she was declared *persona non grata* on the manor in 1275. For a year she lived with two well-to-do widows for whom she worked as a servant, but the following year, having moved away, she stole corn and peas from the widows who had sheltered her, set fire to their house and then fled. There is no record of what happened to Alice after that.

PEASANT LIFE

Peasant wives were full-time workers. They not only shared in the general agricultural labour, but also worked in their own small gardens where they grew vegetables, kept a few chickens and perhaps a pig to improve the family's meagre diet or, more likely, to sell. They would gather herbs and firewood from the common land and do all the domestic tasks of weaving the cloth for the household, cooking and doing the laundry. Above all, they bore, nursed and took care of the children who, as soon as they were able to toddle about, would begin to make their own contribution to the family's labours. Even so, mothers had to keep the little ones close as they went on with their own tasks, and the problems of supervision, as any mother knows, grew more difficult as the babies became toddlers, endlessly curious and with no sense of danger.

Apart from all this housework, many wives were involved in commercial enterprises too, such as brewing, baking or even butchery. Brewing was the main economic activity for women in the villages because ale was a necessary food source and large amounts were drunk. It had to be made

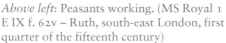

Above left: Peasants working. (MS Royal 1 E IX f. 62v – Ruth, south-east London, first quarter of the fifteenth century)

Above right: An elderly peasant woman. (MS Harley 4425 f. 10v, British Library – Vieillesse, *Roman de la Rose*, Bruges, 1490–1500)

regularly, since hops were not in general use until the late fifteenth century and ale, without this preservative, quickly went sour after a few days. A busy wife could fit the brewing processes in between other activities over several days because they didn't need constant attention. A mash was prepared from crushed malt, (malt is made from steeped and germinated barley grain), added to water and heated in a great pot to convert the starch in the grain to sugar. Yeast and sometimes spices or other flavourings were added before the liquid 'wort' was strained off. This was the strongest brew so it was drunk by the men. Second brewings produced 'small beer' for women, children and servants to drink. The equipment needed was quite basic – large pots, ladles and straining cloths, as well as grain, water and firewood. Poorer peasants could make some extra income from the sale of their ale, but its price was regulated by assize (law). Each village had its own appointed ale-tasters, almost always male, who had to approve the measures used, the quality and pricing of each batch before it went on sale. However, sharp practice was so frequent that the fining of brewsters was almost considered as licence payment. The story of the widow who saved her house from the fire raging around it by lining up all her ale measuring pots at her door and praying that, if she was an honest woman, God would stop the flames, was considered an obvious miracle.

There is a fifteenth-century poem, although it would seem to be based on a much earlier text called the *Ballad of a Tyrannical Husband*, which gives us some idea of how a peasant woman's work was certainly never done for the day:

> The goodman and his lad to the plough are gone,
> The goodwife had much to do, and servant had she none,
> Many small children to look after beside herself alone,
> She did more than she could inside her own house.
>
> Home came the goodman early in the day
> To see that everything was according to his wishes.
> 'Dame,' he said, 'is our dinner ready?' 'Sir,' she said, 'no.
> How would you have me do more than I can?'
>
> Then he began to chide and said, 'Damn you!
> I wish you would go all day to plough with me,
> To walk in the clods that are wet and boggy,
> Then you would know what it is to be a ploughman.'
>
> Then the goodwife swore, and thus she said,
> 'I have more to do than I am able to do.
> If you were to follow me for a whole day,
> You would be weary of your part, I dare bet my head.'

'Blast! In the devil's name!' said the goodman,
'What have you to do, but sit here at home?
You go to your neighbour's house, one after the other,
And sit there chattering with Jack and with Jane.'

The goodwife then tells him how she had hardly any sleep last night because of
the baby, yet she was first up in the morning to milk the cows and take them out
to pasture while he was still asleep. Then she spends the day making butter and
cheese and tending the children. She has to feed the chickens, ducks and geese and
take them onto the green. She bakes and brews and prepares flax for weaving
and teases, cards and spins wool. Her husband then complains that she brews
and bakes more often than necessary – once a fortnight would be enough – she
laughs. She goes on to explain how she makes the linen and woollen cloth for
the family's clothes so they don't have the huge expense of buying cloth from the
market. She also prepares food for the animals

'... And food for ourselves before it is noon,
Yet I don't get a fair word when I have done

So I look to our welfare both outdoors and inside
So that nothing great or small is lacking ...'

For the unfree woman, neither her time nor her person was ever her own, as
specified in these manor court rolls. The first example is from Halesowen in 1300
and the second is from Littleport in 1326.

Day in autumn. The daughter of William de Wylinghurst, two daughters of
Nicholas le Yonge, two daughters of Thomas Colling and the daughter of
Dygan to work two days for the lord in autumn, each of them one day at the
wheat.

And that Mabel Beucosyn absented herself in the autumn and would reap
neither the lord's corn nor her neighbours' for her wages, but went from the vill
against the ordinance of the bylaw.

Christine de Pisan, a Frenchwoman who never had to labour in the fields, has an
idealised image of life for the poor in her *Treasure of the City of Ladies*:

It is not necessary to prohibit fancy ornaments or extravagant clothing to them
(the simple labouring women in the villages), for they are well protected from
these excesses! Although they are commonly raised on black bread, salt pork
and gruel, with only water to drink, and they work very hard, their lives are
more secure and more abundant in essentials than the lives of some who are

placed very high ... As we spoke to all classes of women, it is fitting that we end our work with the class that God loves but the world hates – the poor. We exhort them to patience because of the hope of the crown that is promised them, saying: O blessed poor, by the judgement of God, waiting for the possession of Heaven by the merit of poverty patiently borne, rejoice in this great promise of joy which surpasses everything else ... It is not promised to kings, princes or the rich ...

Christine is almost telling the poor how lucky they are, but it is unlikely that she would swap places with a poor woman even so. It is just as well that such women did not have the ability or opportunity to read Christine's work which would probably not have impressed them.

PEASANTS IN WILLIAM LANGLAND'S *PIERS PLOWMAN*
William Langland uses the image of a shrewish wife in his allegorical story in *Piers Plowman* to represent the wickedness of the flesh. The Samaritan in the story is telling the tale.

> There are three things that make a man by force
> To flee from his own house, as Holy Writ shows.
> The first one is a shrewish wife who will not be chastised;
> Her mate flees her for fear of her tongue ...
> ... The wife is our wicked flesh that will not be chastised
> Because nature cleaves to it to contravene the soul;
> And though it falls it finds excuses that 'Frailty caused it,'
> And 'That is fast forgotten and forgiven too
> To a man who asks for mercy and means to amend.'

Incidentally, the other two causes of a man leaving his home are a leaking roof and a smoking fire but, clearly, a shrewish wife is the most unbearable. Despite the risk of acquiring such a wife, Langland sees marriage as a good thing, if only for the generation of children.

> So widow without wedlock may not well be,
> Nor matrimony without children is not much to be praised
> Thus manhood separate, as a thing by itself, subsists in three persons,
> That is man and his mate and from marriage their children ...

Both Piers Plowman and Langland himself in real life were wed. Langland's wife is mentioned by name in the text, as is his daughter:

> When bells rang for the Resurrection, and right then I awoke
> And called Kit my wife and Calote my daughter:

'Arise and go reverence God's resurrection,
And creep to the Cross on knees, and kiss it as a jewel,
For God's blessed body it bore for our good,
And it frightens the Fiend, for such is its power
That no grisly ghost may glide in its shadow.'

Piers's fictitious wife is Dame-Work-When-It's-Time-To and, when Piers dies, he says, 'My wife shall have what I won with truth, and nothing else, / And parcel it out among my friends and my dear children.' He instructs all wives, peasants or not, when the question is asked,

'What ought we women to work at meanwhile?'
Some shall sew sacks to stop the wheat from spilling …
Wives and widows, spin wool and flax;
Make cloth, I counsel you, and teach the craft to your daughters.
The needy and the naked, take note how they fare:
Keep them from cold with clothing, for so Truth wishes.

From Passus VI we get a good idea of what the peasant wife would be putting on the table for her family until the harvest came in:

I've no penny, said Piers, to purchase pullets,
And I can't get goose or pork; but I've got two green cheeses,
A few curds and cream and a cake of oatmeal,
A loaf of beans and bran baked for my children.
And yet I say, by my soul, I have no salt bacon
Nor any hen's egg, by Christ, to make ham and eggs,
But scallions aren't scarce, nor parsley, and I've scores of cabbages,
And also a cow and a calf, and a cart-mare
To draw dung to the field while the dry weather lasts.
By this livelihood I must live until Lammas time
When I hope to have harvest in my garden.

WOMEN IN MEDIEVAL MYSTERY PLAYS

Medieval mystery plays were biblical pageants, religious in origin but acted out, usually, in the open air. In York, the Corpus Christi pageants were performed annually in celebration of the early summer feast. Each trade guild was responsible for an individual play; for example, the Goldsmiths were responsible for the pageant of the Three Kings with their precious gifts and elaborate costumes. They were responsible for the pageant wagon – the mobile stage on which the play would be performed – the painted scenery, costumes and props, and the actors would normally be members of the guild. The pageant wagons would roll through the city streets in the correct order for the telling of

Medieval Mystery Play at Chester, from the first edition of the *Book of Days* by Robert Chamber (d. 1871).

the biblical story, from the Creation – performed by the Tanners – to the Last Judgement – performed by the Mercers – stopping at specific venues to repeat the plays.

It is said that all the actors were men, even the Virgin Mary, but one 'female' character, perhaps the forerunner of our modern pantomime dames, delighted the audiences with her stubborn, shrewish ways. Although the Bible barely mentions her, Noah's wife came to play quite a prominent part in the pageants. Sometimes, as in the Chester and Towneley cycles of plays, there is one pageant for both the Making of the Ark and the Flood; other times, as in York and Newcastle, the two stories were dealt with separately. The Trinity House Guild of Master Mariners and Pilots in Hull used to act a Noah play on Plough Monday in January.

In Chester, the pageant of Noah's Flood was performed by the Water-Leaders and Drawers in the Dee. Noah's wife, as in the Noah pageants of York and Towneley, is utterly unlike the religious idea of her as a meek and virtuous woman. Instead, in the best English comic tradition, she is a contrary and cantankerous wife, not found in European drama, although she does appear in other art forms and folklore throughout Europe. An early English manuscript has Noah's wife standing at the foot of the gangway to the Ark, one of her sons trying to persuade her to go on board. The following excerpts of dialogue come from the Chester version of Noah's Flood:

Noah and all his family are working with different tools, as though building an ark.

Noah:
Wife in this castle we shall be kept [kept safe];
My children and thou, I would, in leapt ...

Good wife, do now as I thee bid.

Noah's Wife:
By Christ, not ere I see more need,
Though thou stand all day and stare.

Noah:
Lord, that woman be crabbed ay [always perverse],
And never are meek, that dare I say ...

Good wife, let be all this bere [clamour]
That thou makes in this place here;

Wife, come in! Why stands thou there?
Thou art ever forward [perverse], that I dare swear.
Come in, on God's half [for God's sake]! Time it were,
For fear lest that we drown.

Noah's Wife:
Yea, sir, set up your sail,
And row forth with evil hail [bad luck],
For, without any fail [doubt],
I will not out of this town.
But I have my gossips [friends] every one,
One foot further I will not gone ...

Else row forth, Noah, whither thou list [where you please],
And get thee a new wife.

The argument continues, Noah's wife will not leave without her friends and would rather remain behind with them, sharing a two quart pot of strong Malmsey wine.

Mrs Noah in Noah's Ark. (MS Harley 4381 f. 12, British Library – Bible Historiale, France, 1403)

Japheth:
Mother, we pray you altogether –
For we are here your own childer –
Come into the ship for fear of the weather,
For his love that you bought [Your redeemer]!

Noah's Wife:
That will I not, for all your call [bidding],
Whether you will or nought.

(They drag her up the gangplank.)

Noah:
Welcome, wife, into this boat.

Noah's Wife:
And have thou that for thy note [trouble]!

(She boxes his ears)

EFFECTS OF THE BLACK DEATH

In 1348, the great pestilence, as it was called at the time (the Black Death being a later name given to the most terrible scourge known to mankind in the Middle Ages), arrived in England on the Dorset coast at Melcombe Regis. We are not going to discuss the plague itself, but rather the drastic effect it had on the lives of the peasants in the years following. However, we must first think about the situation in England before its catastrophic arrival.

Around the year 1300, the population of England was at its maximum, perhaps between 5 and 6 million – a peak it did not achieve again until Stuart times. This high population meant that areas of crop-growing had been extended to provide food for so many; parts of Dartmoor, for instance, were cultivated, as were other areas of poor soil. Known as marginal land, such areas were literally on the edge of cultivation and subsistence. Where the soil had previously been fertile and productive, it was now over-worked: fields were not allowed to lie fallow to recover and the failure to rotate crops, as had been done in the past, drained the goodness from the earth. Forests were cut down so more land could be cultivated, but demand always outstripped production and, eventually, the wholesale removal of woodland led to less 'free' food being available from the countryside and a shortage of fuel and building material.

With population levels at their highest throughout Europe, the climate then took a hand, plunging the whole area into a 'mini ice age'. The intense cold led to a significant advance of the polar icecap and the alpine glaciers, and high rainfall was dramatic enough to cause a rise in the level of the Caspian Sea. The cultivation of cereal crops in Iceland was no longer possible, neither was the growing of vines in much of England. The wheat-growing areas of Scandinavia and the French upland regions were greatly reduced. The worst result of this climate change was a series of disastrous famines. Between 1315 and 1319, almost every country in Europe lost virtually the whole of one harvest, often two or three. The lack of sunshine hindered the ripening of grain and fruits, as well as the production of salt by evaporation, which was the most common and cheapest method of making it. Since salt was vital for preserving meat, this too was also quickly in short supply. In England, wheat more than doubled in price and peasants, so it was recorded, were reduced to eating cats and dogs, even children, according to one chronicler. 10 per cent of the population of Ypres died of starvation in one famine year.

1332 was another year of disastrous crop failure, as were the years 1345–48, which might have been noted as the catastrophe of the century, had it not been for the events that followed. Therefore, even before the arrival of the Black Death, the economies of Europe were in recession. Put in the simplest terms, Europe had outgrown its own strength and the entire population was at its weakest just when it was about to face its most devastating challenge. Of course, the poor were the most malnourished of all and, therefore, the least able to fight infection.

We all know that the population of England was devastated by the Black Death, suffering horrors we can hardly imagine. What isn't always realised is that the plague

Ploughman. (MS Burney 272 f. 18, British Library – Germany, 1473)

recurred regularly after its first horrendous visitation, further outbreaks occurring in 1361 – this occasion causing almost as severe loss of life, especially among children, as the first – 1368–69, 1371, 1375, 1390 and 1405. In fact, England was never entirely free of the plague for the next three centuries, which meant that the population never had a chance to regain its former size. The result for the peasants was that they were suddenly, for the first time ever, a commodity in short supply. Landowners were desperate for their labour services and, so long as the land was worked, food was now more than sufficient to go around the much reduced population.

Peasants began to demand higher wages. On the manor lands of Cuxham in Oxfordshire, a ploughman had earned 2s a year before the plague, but in 1349–50 he earned 7s and by 1351 received as much as 10s 6d. On top of this, food prices fell – the peasant was suddenly better off! As regards women, like the menfolk, their labour was in greater demand but, where the type of employment allowed, their work was suddenly preferred to that of men because they could be paid considerably less for the same job. This was necessary for landowners whose rents had decreased through the death of tenants, and the profits from selling grain and other food crops had fallen so dramatically that it was impossible to pay labourers the higher wages they demanded. The price of manufactured goods actually rose at this time because there were fewer skilled artisans to produce them and again women, particularly the widows, stepped in to fill the breach, making better profits than before. However, the somewhat better-paid peasants could now afford the odd little luxury item here and there which resulted in a boom in trade for things like items of personal jewellery, leather goods and the occasional piece of quality furniture. Peasants had become 'consumers'.

However, naturally, the landowning classes disapproved of any new freedoms for the peasants and the law stepped in to try to rectify the matter very swiftly. The Ordinance of Labourers in 1349 and the Statute of Labourers in 1351 were intended to keep wages down and prevent workmen transferring their loyalties to someone willing to pay better wages than their present employer. These laws did have an effect, but couldn't prevent the medieval labourer from realising he had a value in society, a right to decide his terms of employment and to seek his fortune elsewhere if that right was denied him. The decisive role played by the humble longbowmen of England in winning the battles of Crecy (1346) and Poitiers (1356) also raised the peasants' awareness of their own worth: the king could not do without them.

In William Langland's work, it is Piers Plowman himself who complains of the greed and laziness of labourers. Farmers and peasants with larger plots and less help than before the Black Death had more need of labour beyond what their own family could provide, so there was no lack of work for anyone in the village. Neither was there any lack of work elsewhere. Consequently, the late Middle Ages became a time of great mobility in rural areas. It wasn't just the wage labourers that were involved for, in many communities, there was plenty of land waiting to be worked where previous tenants had died and there was no one to replace them. From the late fourteenth until well into the fifteenth century, there is plenty of evidence in the manorial court rolls that lords were having difficulties in finding takers for vacant tenements, especially if the soil was poor. The peasants were becoming choosy about which land was worth their efforts to cultivate and which lord would make a good master.

The most dramatic outcome of this new way of thinking for the peasants of England was the occurrence of the Peasants' Revolt in 1381. Unfortunately, all the promises made to Wat Tyler and his peasant army by King Richard II concerning their grievances were all refuted within a couple of days, once the crowds had dispersed to their homes. However, the situation for the poor could never be quite as it had been before the Black Death and, gradually, little by little, they got the freedoms they demanded: the right to leave the manor where they were born; to seek higher wages elsewhere and to pay money in lieu of services rendered to the lord of the manor.

MANOR COURT ROLLS

Peasant women had some private rights and could inherit property in default of direct male heirs. They might also have customary rights, which varied greatly from manor to manor, in their husband's property after his death. For a peasant woman, as for other women, her legal status was defined by her marital status but, in any case, there were likely to be few female tenants. For an example from Kent, the 'Rental Roll of the Manor of Meltone (Milton) by Gravesende, made by the tenants on the morrow of St Hilary, in the sixteenth year of the reign of King Richard II' (1393) shows that of at least fifty-two tenants (some are listed as 'the heirs of …' so we know simply that there was more than one tenant), only one, Sabina Stace, is female, most probably a widow.

The Manor Court Rolls for Tottenham in 1395 give an example of a bondswoman given the holding of a tenement, at least until her son is old enough to inherit it, with the following terms and conditions:

To this court has come Alice, late wife of Thomas Ederych and receives of the lord the tenure of five acres and three roods of land to hold to herself until the legal age of John, the youngest son of the aforesaid Thomas, who, according to the custom of the manor, will inherit the land in bondage, and the aforesaid Alice is to keep the said John, who is now six years of age, in food and clothing well and competently until his legal age, and she gives to the lord a fine for entry 2s and does fealty, and she pledges John Malton and Thomas Fynch. And after the full age of the said heir, if she shall have kept herself sole and in good repute without husband, then she shall have the said tenement and lands for her whole life, and if she shall not, then it is to be taken into the lord's hands according to the custom of the manor.

At the Court of Bradford, held on Thursday 11 March 1350, various peasant women were having to pay the fines: *leyrwite*, a fine paid for fornication or for bearing an illegitimate child; *merchet*, a fine paid by a woman for the lord's permission to marry; and *chevage*, an annual payment made by a serf for the privilege of living away from manor lands.

> Alice Chilyonge of Manningham, the lord's bondwoman, came here in court and made fine of 12*d* with the lord for her leyrwite; pledge, William Walker; and the fine is not more because she is very poor and has nothing.

> It is presented that Isobel daughter of William Childyong, the lord's bondwoman, has married one William Cisson, a free man, without licence. And Alice daughter of John Gepson, the lord's bondwoman, has married one William del Hale, a free man, at Beston, without licence; therefore let them be distrained to make fine with their lord for their merchet, etc.

> Agnes daughter of Adam atte Yate, the lord's bondwoman, has made her fine for chevage, for licence to dwell wheresoever she will, to wit, 6*d* to be paid yearly at Michaelmas and Easter in equal proportions; pledge, Robert atte Yate.

Other, rather sad, events in the lives of peasant women are recorded in the rolls of various coroners' courts. These incidents occurred in Bedfordshire but are reflected in the rolls of many other counties:

> On 14th January 1267 Sabillia, an old woman, went into Colmworth to beg bread. At twilight she wished to go to her house, fell into a stream and drowned by misadventure. The next day her son Henry searched for her and found her drowned.

> About prime on 27th March 1270 Mariot, formerly the wife of Richard the Reeve of Pertenhall, who was infirm, feeble and old, lay in her bed in Pertenhall while Maud Mody, John Spayne and Richard's son Henry were about the affairs of the house, at the plough and elsewhere. She rose from her bed, took a pitcher in her hand, went to a well in her courtyard and tried to draw water, but, because she was feeble, she slipped and fell into the well and drowned by misadventure. Maud Mody came to the house and into the courtyard, saw Mariot lying in the well and raised the hue. John Speyne came to the hue and sprang to Mariot, because he thought to save her, but could not because she was dead.

These frail, elderly women met similar ends but in quite different circumstances: the one, having to beg her bread, out all alone after dark; the other cared for in a comfortable home with its own well in the courtyard, the widow of the reeve (an office that predates that of 'mayor') and rather better off, though still classed as a peasant. However, misfortune could befall younger women too – this next incident also gives us an insight into life at home:

> About prime on 28th February (no year given but probably 1270 or 71), while William Sagar of Sutton was at the plough, his wife Emma took a bundle of straw inside the courtyard of his house in Sutton, intending to go to heat an oven. She came to a part of the courtyard which was near their dwelling house and near a well on the north side of the house, and by misadventure fell into the well and drowned. Maud daughter of Ellis Batte of Sutton was sitting in William's house guarding Emma's child Rose, who was lying in a cradle, heard the noise made by Emma as she sank, immediately went outside and found Emma drowned.

The unfortunate Emma clearly lived in a reasonable house with a courtyard and well, like Mariot in the previous extract, but she also had her own oven, which not everyone did, and seems to have employed a neighbour's daughter to baby sit. But baby-minding seems to have brought its own risks, as this last entry shows:

> At twilight on 4th September 1300 Nicholas le Swon of Bedford came to his house there, when his wife Isabel was at Robert Asplon's house giving milk to Robert's son, and asked his daughter where her mother was. She said: at Robert Asplon's house; whereupon he immediately went after her because she stayed there too much. As he left his house he met his wife and told her to come home to sleep, saying that he wanted to go to his bed. While Isabel was making his bed, Nicholas drew his sword and struck her in the back so that she immediately died. He immediately fled.

Adam and Eve working with Cain and Abel behind. (MS Harley 2838 f5, British Library, London, 1485)

5

Medieval Ladies

In the medieval world of literature, the upper class lady was important as the ideal in chivalry where she was the beloved one, the source of all romance and inspiration and the object of worship. She had but to command and would be obeyed; only for her all deeds of valour would be performed. More realistically, in law and in feudal society, she was primarily important as a landowner. In the family, she was important as a wife and mother, wielding practical authority, not only in her own domestic sphere, but in a much wider one as her husband's representative during his absence.

However, the term 'ladies' covers a considerable range of women from various social groups: everyone from duchesses to lesser gentry. A lady might improve her status through an advantageous marriage, or even a series of marriages, adding to her wealth and giving access to new networks of local importance. These ladies understood power and weren't shy of using it. Although a noblewoman might be the heiress of a title and the lands and riches that went with it, it would be her husband, during their marriage, who took over the title, the wealth and the duties that it involved. During marriage, the wife was usually occupied with the supervision of the household and, if the husband was absent, of the estates as well, but also with the bearing and upbringing of the children. Real power for a noble woman, as for those of other social classes, came with widowhood when she took full control of her dower lands and, frequently, if the heir was a minor, the management and supervision of all the lands and revenues until he came of age.

A queen and her ladies. (MS Royal 16 G V f. 3v British Library – *Le livre de femmes nobles et renomées*, Rouen, France, 1440)

Widows might still, occasionally, be forced into subsequent marriages by royal command (although Magna Carta forbade this), but many widows who could afford it bought their right to remain single or choose their next husband from the Crown. A letter from Queen Margaret of Anjou, wife of Henry VI in the later fifteenth century, suggests the pattern for royal coercion in such cases. The queen wrote to Dame Jane Carew, a widow with a moderate inheritance of seventeen manors, to persuade her to look favourably on a marriage proposal from Margaret's squire, remarking rather ominously that compliance would improve her standing with the queen. Dame Carew refused, purchased a licence from the Bishop of Exeter and made a very profitable marriage with the Earl of Oxford's brother instead.

By the late fourteenth and fifteenth centuries, the daughters and widows of wealthy London merchants began to be considered as suitable marriage partners for the upper class man, since merchant wealth could be considerable and was welcomed by the impoverished noble families. The remarriage of London merchants' widows might take them up the social scale in leaps and bounds, as the case of Matilda Frauncey's illustrates. She was the daughter of an important fourteenth-century London alderman and married three times. Her first husband was John Aubrey, a rich young merchant; her second, Sir Alan Buxhall, was Keeper of the Tower of London and a Knight of the Garter; and her third was the ill-fated John Montague, Earl of Salisbury, executed for treason in 1400.

Above left: A knight's lady at England's Medieval Festival, Herstmonceux, 2014. (Pat Patrick)

Above right: Margaret of Anjou and her son, Prince Edward, in the Luxembourg Gardens, Paris. The inscription on the statue reads, translated, 'If you do not respect a proscribed queen, respect an unhappy mother.' (Deborah Esrick)

His unfortunate end did not affect the social successes of Matilda's children, as her son married the co-heiress of the Earl of Kent and all her daughters married noblemen, one attracting the Duke of Exeter as her third husband.

Widows were common in noble families but spinsters were virtually unknown. Girls who could not be wed – either for the lack of a dowry or because of some mental or physical disability – were normally placed in a convent before they became an embarrassment as a spinster. Otherwise, they remained in their family's care while marriage negotiations were actively underway. An example of the twists and turns of some marriage negotiations is seen in the case of Agnes, the little daughter of Henry of Essex, beginning sometime in the 1150s.

The 1st Earl of Oxford, Aubrey de Vere, in the mid-twelfth century, had married twice and was in his forties but still had no heir. Meanwhile, a marriage was being arranged by his brother, Geoffrey de Vere, and Henry of Essex, an important royal official and great landowner under Henry II, for Geoffrey and Henry's three-year-old daughter, Agnes, to be wed. With the marriage agreement settled, at the age of six, Agnes moved into Geoffrey's household and (so Geoffrey alleged) was treated with all the honour due to his future wife. It was later claimed that she had agreed to the betrothal but the girl herself steadfastly denied this. In 1162, when she was eleven or twelve – on the verge of the age of consent – the earl, Aubrey de Vere, betrothed himself to her, displacing his brother as prospective bridegroom.

Then, in 1163, her father, Henry of Essex, fell out of favour with the king and forfeited his power, privileges and estates. Suddenly, Agnes's value in the marriage market was gone. According to the rules of aristocratic society, great men married for the benefit of their estates – good breeding stock begetting heirs, bringing dowries and desirable family alliances. Agnes was no longer desirable and the de Veres expected to be able to set her aside. However, the laws concerning marriage were administered by the Church and subject to the Church's doctrines. This did not necessarily make much difference but, in Agnes's case, it did.

Wedding. (MS Harley 4380 f. 6, British Library – Chroniques, Vol. IV, part 2, Bruges, 1470)

Agnes was only twelve and the de Veres thought nothing of her interest in the matter but she was not to be disposed of so easily. She must have had friends in high places to help her – we don't know who they were – and she clearly had an exceptional degree of courage and determination and was prepared to put up with almost anything to save her own and her family's name. Agnes got a hearing in the court of Gilbert Foliot, the Bishop of London, and the de Veres were forced to fight their case. The Church insisted on the consent of *both* parties in a marriage. The earl, his brother Geoffrey and the girl's father had all supposed that marriage in aristocratic society was simply a treaty drawn up by the parents; handing over the girl as a virtual hostage was, for them, the crucial act. Consent meant nothing under these circumstances.

However, the bishop thought it safest to take his time over coming to a decision, not wishing to upset either the de Veres or the king. Agnes and her advocates had little trust in the fair dealing to be expected in an English court anyway, so she appealed to Rome. That was in 1166 and, though the matter rumbled on, little happened for the next five or six years. Meanwhile, the earl shut Agnes up in a tower and treated her abominably in the hope she would admit defeat. She was a very determined young lady and seems to have had a talent for melting the hearts of those in distant high places. At first, the Pope was in no more hurry than the bishop but, in the end, he appears to have been deeply moved by accounts he received both of her plight and her determination to uphold the Church's regard for the act of consent.

At the end of January 1172, the Pope sent a mandate to Bishop Foliot stating that

> The earl is to take her back as his wife, to treat her with due respect, to share his table and his bed with her as husband and wife; and he is to do this within twenty days of the arrival of this mandate or the bishop is to lay an interdict on his lands and to excommunicate the earl himself. Dated at Frascati, thirtieth day of January 1171–2.

The bishop obeyed, the earl complied and the marriage of Aubrey and Agnes was consummated. Her heroic stand had a successful ending, though whether it also had a happy one

Two ladies at the Battle of Tewkesbury re-enactment, 2014. (Pat Patrick)

we cannot know. He was about sixty years old by this time and she was just over twenty but, since he lived until 1194, they raised at least five children from whom all the later de Veres, Earls of Oxford, were descended. This family were to become the longest continuous line of English earls. It was a most inauspicious beginning to an aristocratic marriage and shows the harshness of contemporary custom coming into conflict with the Church. The Church didn't always win, either, but at least, in Agnes's case, it had supported the woman, so often regarded as of little account by both custom and the Church.

CHAUCER'S *THE BOOK OF THE DUCHESSE*

For a view of what medieval men expected of the perfect lady, we can turn to one of Chaucer's early poems. *The Book of the Duchess* is a dream-vision, a poetic form Chaucer used in some of his other works too, like *The Parliament of Fowls*. The poem was most likely written as a consolation piece for the bereaved John of Gaunt and a celebration of the life of his duchess, Blanche of Lancaster, being both tactful and indirect. The meeting with the knight in mourning black and his story of his dead lady, White (Blanche), occur within a dream sequence, the characters only identified obliquely at the end of the poem.

> With that, me thoghte, that this king
> Gan quikly hoomward for to ryde [began]
> Unto a place ther besyde,
> Which was from us but a lyte [little],
> A long castel with walles whyte,
> By seynt Johan! On a riche hil,
> As me mette; but thus it fil [as I reckon or measure; befell, happened]

The 'long castel' is a pun on Lancaster. St John refers to John of Gaunt himself and 'riche hil' may refer to Richmond, as Gaunt was Earl of Richmond in his own right, as well as Duke of Lancaster in right of his wife. The knight's description of the lady, White, is lengthy, taking up a fair proportion of the poem and includes most of the conventional attributes of a perfect lady: she is tall and slim with fair shoulders, white hands, rounded breasts, her hair is like gold and her throat is like a tower of ivory. She is Nature's supreme example of her art, yet the knight is more concerned to describe the lady's goodness than her beauty:

> ... my lady swete ...
> That was so fayr, so fresh, so free,
> So good, that men may wel y-see
> Of al goodnesse she had no mete [equal]!

White's face is not only beautiful but 'stedfast', which means that it maintains a perfect poise between gravity and joyfulness, moderation in all things being the ideal.

More than once, this paragon of womanhood is described as 'sadde', but in Middle English this word had alternative meanings to today's word. Rather than 'sorrowful' the word suggests she took things as seriously as they required. Today, it is harder for us to understand how this quality of sadness exists alongside a radiant happiness, which is equally virtuous. She sings, dances, laughs and plays 'so womanly':

> I saw hir daunce so comlily,
> Carole and singe so swetely,
> Laughe and pleye so womanly,
> And loke so debonairly,
> So goodly speke and frendly,
> That certes, I trow [I believe], that evermore
> Nas seyn so blisful a tresore [treasure].

Her name, 'White' (a play on the duchess's name, Blanche), also applies to her lover's belief that she was his torch in the darkness: 'To derke ys turned al my lyght,' he says sadly of her passing. Her name also provides the contrast to the knight as the 'man in black', her happiness with his mourning and the grief of the other characters in the poem. Important to her perfection, despite the admiration attracted by her great beauty, the lady is not in the least flirtatious and, although she has great power, has no desire to make use of it. Such was the medieval ideal of the perfect lady, but few ever attained such perfection: Eve was a more likely template than the Virgin Mary for the ladies as described by medieval poets.

The lady of chivalry was always a beautiful yet artificial creature, never the figure of a real person but, just occasionally, we do get a glimpse in the original sources of real, flesh and blood women. One such comes from the *Book of the Reformation of Monasteries* (1470 – 75) by Johann Busch, a German priest, in which he recalls the dying confession of the Duchess of Brunswick:

When her confession with absolution and penance was ended, I said to her 'think you, lady, that you will pass to the kingdom of heaven when you die?' She replied 'this believe I firmly.' Said I 'that would be a marvel. You were born in a fortress and bred in castles and for many years now you have lived with your husband, the lord duke, ever in the midst of manifold delights, with wine and ale, meat and venison; and yet you expect to fly away to heaven directly you die.' She answered 'beloved father, why should I not now go to heaven? I have lived here in this castle like an anchoress in a cell. What delights or pleasures have I enjoyed here, save that I have made shift to show a happy face to my servants and gentlewomen? I have a hard husband (as you know) who has scarce any care or inclination towards women. Have I not been in this castle even as it were in a cell?'

Perhaps, in reality, the ladies of the chivalric romances spent a life of boredom and isolation from the world like the Duchess of Brunswick but, of course, this

A medieval lady at the Battle of Bosworth re-enactment, 2014. (Pat Patrick)

was not the idealistic picture that male authors describe.

MALORY'S *MORTE D'ARTHUR*

Thomas Malory, the fifteenth-century author of the compilation of tales of King Arthur and his knights, the *Morte d'Arthur*, first printed by William Caxton in 1485, sees all damsels and ladies as beautiful – outwardly at least – but, without exception, they are out to deceive men in one way or another. Seeing women as the daughters of Eve, rather than the sisters of the Virgin Mary, was the usual stance of the Catholic church during the later Middle Ages though, on rare occasions, authors do give us the alternative image, as we saw in *The Book of the Duchess* above. Ladies abound in the *Morte d'Arthur* but most appear fleetingly and are creatures of little character. One of the few ladies who are sinned against, occurs in the first chapter of Book I. She is the Lady Igrayne, wife of the Duke of Tintagel, to whom King Uther Pendragon has taken a fancy. In fact, the king has fallen madly in love with the 'fayr' Igrayne, but she remains true to her lord and it will require the use of magic for the love-sick Uther to get into the lady's bed. This is accomplished when Merlin gives Uther the appearance and form of the Duke of Tintagel. The lady accepts him as her husband, later to discover that, at the time, her husband had already been slain in battle, but, for the sake of the child she now bears, the good lady 'mourned pryvely and held hir pees'.

This same trick is tried again with Sir Lancelot and the Lady Elaine (Book XI). This time, the Lady Elaine, the king's daughter, is caused to appear as Queen Guinevere to Lancelot's eyes, in order to complete a prophesy that the knight should beget a son, Galahad, upon her. It is Dame Brusen, a great enchantress, who persuades King Pelles to allow her to bring this about:

'Sir, wyte you well Sir Launcelot lovyth no lady in the worlde but all only Quene Gwenyver. And therefore worche ye be [be guided by] my counceyle, And I shall make hym to lye wyth youre doughter, and he shall nat wyte [know] but that he lyeth by quene Gwenyver.'

And than dame Brusen brought sir Launcelot a kuppe of wyne, and anone as he had drunken that wyne he was so asoted [infatuated] and madde that he myght make no delay but wythoute ony let [hindrance] he wente to bedde. And so he wente [believed] that mayden Elayne had bene quene Gwenyver. And wyte [know] you well that sir Launcelot was glad, and so was that lady Elayne that she had gotyn sir Launcelot in her armys, for well she knew that same nyght sholde be bygotyn sir Galahad uppon her, that sholde preve [prove] the beste knyght of the worlde.

Lancelot and Guinevere. (MS Additional 10293 f 199, British Library – Lancelot du Lac, Tournai, Belgium, 1316)

However, the light of day breaks the spell and Lancelot realises what he has done and calls the lady a traitoress and says that she will die by his hands. Elaine, stark naked, falls on her knees before him, begging for mercy, flattering him as 'the moste noble knyght of the worlde'. When she reveals that she is the daughter of King Pelles and all was done in fulfilment of a prophesy, Lancelot forgives her. Besides, as the lady points out,

> … to fullfyll this prophecie I have gyvyn the [thee] the grettyst ryches and the fayryst floure that ever I had, and that is my maydynhode that I shall never have agayne. And therefore, jantyll knyght, owghe [owe] me youre good wyll.

However, despite the deceit that was practised upon him, when Queen Guinevere hears tales of what he has been up to there is no forgiveness from her (Book XVIII):

> 'Sir Launcelot, now I well understonde that thou arte a false, recrayed [cowardly] knyght and a comon lechourere, and lovyste and holdiste othir ladyes, and of me thou haste dysdayne and scorne. For wyte [know] thou well, now I undirstonde thy falsehede I shall never love the [thee] more, And loke thou be never so hardy [daring] to com into my syght. And right here I dyscharge the[thee] thys courte, that thou never com within hit, and I forfende [deny] the my felyship, and uppon payne of thy hede that thou see me nevermore!'

This is more like the beautiful lady with a heart of stone that we have come to expect from the medieval tales of chivalry and romance, but what of real ladies? Let us turn now to the lives of flesh and blood noblewomen.

Ladies join
the parade at
the Battle of
Tewkesbury
re-enactment,
2014. (Pat Patrick)

THE CASE OF JULIANA GAYTON

Unfortunately, women of all social classes could be beaten by their husbands quite legally. The Church approved, regarding women as such morally weak creatures that physical punishment was required to help them see the error of their ways. The only stipulation was that the stick used to beat the erring wife should be no thicker than the husband's thumb. Occasionally, as still happens rarely today, a wife could bear no more and since divorce on the grounds of cruelty to the woman was virtually unknown, the only escape could be considerably more drastic.

The most extreme measure a woman could take was, of course, murder. One lady who was accused of killing her husband was Juliana Gayton, widow of Thomas Murdak, lord of Compton in Warwickshire and Edgecote in Northamptonshire. The Murdaks were a long-established family in both counties. Thomas succeeded his brother to the title in 1298–99. He was already married to Juliana, one of the daughters, and ultimately co-heiresses, of Sir Philip de Gayton of Gayton in Northamptonshire. Their son, John, was seventeen when his father was murdered so it seems that Thomas and Juliana had been wed for many years when their marriage came to an abrupt end.

The murder occurred on Monday 11 April 1316, during Easter week, after dark at Stourton Castle in the Kinver Forest. After the murder, his body, headless and cut into quarters, was left at his manor of Edgecote, presumably expecting that the coroner's inquest would conclude that he had been killed there. It seems to have been some time before any action was taken but, by Michaelmas 1318, Juliana and two co-defendants, Alice le Chaumberere and Adam le Sompter (a sumpter was a packhorse so, presumably, Adam was a groom of some kind) were summonsed to appear in court. Both servants had already been found guilty of failing to appear previously in answer to four successive summonses. For this, Adam was outlawed and both Lady Juliana and the serving-woman received the female equivalent – they were waived. From the names of the co-defendants, it seems likely that the murder was a domestic crime and this is supported by later developments.

In this case, the ancient action of appeal (prosecution) was made by an 'approver', Robert Ruggele of Yelvertoft, who turned king's evidence in an attempt to save himself from the gallows by undertaking to secure the conviction of his associates in crime. Robert named six other persons involved in the murder of Thomas Murdak, in addition to Juliana and himself. He said that the first blow had been struck by William Bodekisham who had struck Thomas on the head with a staff as he lay asleep in bed. When the victim had tried to rise, Robert the Chaplain had stabbed him with a dagger, 'up to the hilt'. Robert the Chaplain was Thomas's household steward, in charge of finances. The fatal action was then committed by Roger the Chamberlain who cut him open above the navel. Roger is described as Juliana's chamberlain, another important member of the household, so it seems the actual perpetrators of the murder were the knight's own principal household servants. Robert Ruggele also incriminated William Shene, the cook, and Adam le Sumpter again, though Alice le Chamberere is not mentioned this time.

Was Juliana the instigator of this crime? Had she persuaded the household servants or did they have reasons of their own to hate their lord? Might they have witnessed his cruelty towards both his wife and themselves once too often? We do know that Juliana was able to persuade men when it mattered to her. The Sheriff of Warwickshire rescinded his waiving (outlawing) of Juliana, having been informed by the Sheriff of Staffordshire that he now had her in his custody, yet this turned out to be blatantly untrue, the Sheriff of Staffordshire having connived at her escape. Later, when the Sheriff of Warwickshire *did* have Juliana in custody, he failed to produce her at the King's Bench on five occasions, saying she was pregnant and too ill to appear without causing harm either to herself or the child she carried. In fact, the sheriff himself had smuggled her across the county border into Leicestershire, to his manor of Shilton where 'she wandered at her will out of prison'. Finally, on the sixth occasion, threatened with imprisonment or fines himself, the sheriff produced Juliana in court on 4 October 1320 and she was committed to the Marshalsea prison in London.

She denied the charge of murdering her husband and a jury of twenty-four, of whom twelve were knights 'girt with a sword', was summoned for 20 January 1321. They reached their verdict by Friday 23 January: on oath they said that Juliana had feloniously and insidiously killed Thomas, who was formally her husband. She was sentenced to be burned, her crime being defined as 'petty treason', but the records of the royal chancery suggest that she was actually hanged.

The murder of Thomas Murdak had clearly been premeditated, but by whom? There is a further dimension to this crime – what was the Murdak household doing at Stourton Castle? This residence belonged to Sir John de Vaux, Keeper of Kinver Forest, and he was there, in the castle, at the time of the murder. Robert de Yelvertoft, who named his partners in crime, was a de Vaux servant and he said that Sir John had commanded and sent him to do the dastardly deed. Juliana had merely abetted the crime – Sir John de Vaux had been the instigator! He had been arrested in London and kept in the custody of the Constable of the Tower. It was revealed that Sir John had married Juliana on Thursday 15 April 1316, just three days after the murder of Thomas, her husband. He was tried by the same jury that sat in judgement on Juliana but he pleaded 'benefit of clergy'. It took a further three years before the verdict was finally delivered; John de Vaux was found not guilty of the said death and of procuring or abetting it. He was therefore acquitted.

The least that can be said of the case is that the jury gave de Vaux the benefit of the doubt. The jury which convicted Juliana was also, of course, all male. Of all the defendants in the case, of whom there were at least fifteen, she was the only one to suffer the full penalty. The differences in the ways Juliana and de Vaux were treated show that their crimes were regarded very differently by the male jurors. A man slaying another is one thing but a woman killing her lord husband is quite another, particularly when there is the suspicion of sexual immorality and adultery as well. A dim view was taken of such a crime by a male-dominated society forever wary of women and their feminine wiles.

ELEANOR DE MONTFORT, COUNTESS OF LEICESTER

Christine de Pisan has a very precise definition of the titles due to aristocratic ladies, as she sets out who are regarded as princesses and who are not in her *Treasure of the City of Ladies*. In France, Eleanor de Montfort, sister to King Henry III of England but wife to a mere Earl of Leicester, would have been called a 'princess' but, in England, the title was not used of royal ladies until Tudor times. What is unclear is what these titles meant as Christine de Pisan saw them. What this extract from her writing shows is how precisely a lady's position in society had to be defined in order that the laws of manners and etiquette were not broken:

Now it is time to talk of ladies and maidens who live in castles or in other manor houses on their estates or in walled towns or cities. We must consider what we can say that may be useful to them. Since their status and powers are different, it behoves us to speak differently about certain things, that is the rank, style and regulation of their lives. But as for habits and good works towards God, everything applies to them that has been said before, to both princesses and court ladies – in short, to cultivate the virtues and shun the vices. There are many powerful ladies who live in various lordships, like baronesses and great landowners, who, however, are not designated princesses. This name 'princess' does not properly apply to any save empresses, queens and duchesses, except the wives of those who, because of their lands, are called princes by the right conferred by the name of the place, as happens in Italy and elsewhere. Although countesses may not be called princesses in all countries, we will consider them to be numbered among the princesses described above, since they follow closely the rank of duchess according to the dignity of the lands.

During Eleanor de Montfort's time, there were no dukes and duchesses in England anyway, such titles being considered a French affectation. Only the king still liked to style himself 'Duke of Normandy' and that was, of course, a French title anyway. Not until the reign of Edward III do we have English dukes and duchesses, when the king decided that his sons were the equals of any French duke whom they were fighting against in what would become known as the Hundred Years War, and so the title began with the royal family. This also solved the problem of mere earls and barons (English) taking dukes (French) as prisoners to be held to ransom. The etiquette of chivalry demanded that captives should be taken only by their equals to avoid humiliation.

Eleanor, the daughter of King John and sister to Henry III, was married for the first time at the age of nine, in the hopes of ensuring the loyalty of her husband, Earl William Marshal the younger. Once married, the woman had a recognised legal position; though her lands and goods were theoretically under her husband's control, she was, in this case, the equal of a man in all matters of private law:

> The woman can hold land, even by military tenure, can own chattels, make a will, make a contract, can sue and be sued. She sues and is sued in person without the interposition of a guardian; she can plead with her own voice if she pleases; indeed – and this is a strong case – a married woman will sometimes appear as her husband's attorney. A widow will often be the guardian of her own children; a lady will often be the guardian of the children of her tenants.
>
> Frederick Maitland

How different the woman's position seems to have been in private law, as opposed to criminal law, though matters did not always work out that way in practice. However, the best evidence for the independence and initiative of women is found in the numerous court cases in which they appear. Eleanor was widowed at the age of about fifteen and her legal struggle for her full dower rights of one-third of her husband's estates, dragged on for over forty years. Despite these legal difficulties and the fact that, after Earl William died, she took a perpetual vow of chastity in the presence of the saintly Archbishop of Canterbury, Eleanor married a second time. Never a lady to conform to the traditional views of morals and manners, she fell in love with a virtually penniless French place-seeker at the English court – Simon de Montfort. She brought her new husband great wealth, even without her dower, and great prestige because she was the king's sister.

Ruins of
Odiham Castle,
Hampshire.
(BabelStone)

Not only was she a lady of importance in her own right, she was also an assertive woman, not meek and submissive as praised by the clerics of the day. The Franciscan friar, Adam Marsh, had occasion to write to her, telling her that she should lay aside all contentions and irritating quarrels and act in a spirit of moderation when she had to counsel her husband. It seems Eleanor was more than capable of having a fierce argument if she didn't get her own way. Obviously a high-spirited woman, she was also unfailingly loyal to her husband, Earl Simon, through good times and bad, whatever their private quarrels. She went with him on his travels to Italy, France and Gascony and some of her children were born abroad – but she was also quite capable of handling the de Montfort concerns alone, whether business or political. The evidence of her household accounts shows the countess was frequently in charge. When the earl was away on campaign, the management of all their affairs was in Eleanor's hands. Items in the accounts show how much political initiative she displayed, who was invited as a guest and how lavish their entertainment should be, and how she used her power, ability and practical foresight to do what was best for her family.

During a trip from Odiham in Hampshire to the greater safety of Dover, at a time when her husband was in arms against the king, she entertained the burgesses of Winchelsea. Only three days after arriving at Dover, she invited the burgesses of nearby Sandwich to dinner and both groups were again invited to Dover Castle a few weeks later. Her purpose is obvious; the loyalty of the townsfolk of the Cinque Ports was crucial to Earl Simon's cause. They guarded the coast against French invasion and could keep out the mercenaries recruited for the king's cause overseas, so Eleanor needed to maintain their friendship.

After the earl's defeat and death at the Battle of Evesham in 1265, Eleanor's role was even more important and demanding as the responsibility for salvaging any fragment of the de Montfort fortunes was hers alone. The accounts show that she wrote endless letters to her unforgiving brother, the king, and pleaded, with greater success, to her other brother, Richard of Cornwall, to ensure his good will and promise of assistance. She arranged the escape of her youngest son to Bigorre and succeeded in smuggling 11,000 marks over to France to support her sons in exile. In a final agreement made at Dover with the king's son, the Lord Edward (later Edward I), Eleanor ensured the return to grace and favour of most of her household, though she herself had to leave the kingdom. All these achievements illustrate her great ability to organise and an incredible capacity for planning. She was not at all the docile, submissive little lady that chivalry expected.

A medieval woman at Corfe Medieval Village, 2014. (Pat Patrick)

6

Women's Dress and Fashion

Before examining medieval fashions, we have to realise just how important 'status' or 'estate' was at this time. It was firmly believed that society would be in total chaos if everyone didn't know and keep to their allotted place in the scheme of things, as God Himself had ordained; a lord was a lord and a peasant was a peasant and evermore shall be so! Sumptuary Laws were evolved to deal with this problem officially but, as you might expect, they were constantly ignored, particularly by the rising merchant class and, as fashion in dress, food, travel, etc. changed, the laws had to be changed as well to cover new styles, new textiles and new ideas, but generally in vain. Below is an excerpt from the English Sumptuary Laws of 1363. It seems that they were still on the statute book in 1810 and may be there even today ... ignored by one and all as they ever were.

Item 8. For the outrageous and excessive apparel of divers people, against their estate and degree, to the great destruction and impoverishment of all the land, it is ordained, that grooms, as well servants of lords, as they of mysteries [regulated craftsmen], and artificers, shall be served to eat and drink once a day of flesh and fish, and the remnant of other victuals, as of milk, butter and cheese, according to their estate. And that they have clothes ... whereof the whole cloth shall not exceed two marks ... not nothing of gold or silver embroidered, aimeled [enamelled], nor of silk. ... Their wives, daughters and children shall be of the same condition ... and they shall wear no veils passing 12 pence a veil.

Item 9. Yeomen and the like shall not wear cloth costing more than 40s, nor gemstone, nor cloth of silk nor of silver, nor girdle, knife, button, ring, garter nor owche [brooch], ribbon, chains, nor no such other things of gold nor of silver, nor no manner of apparel embroidered, aimeled, nor of silk by no way ... wives and daughters to wear no veil of silk, but only of yarn made within the Realm, nor no manner of fur, nor of budge, but only of lamb, cony [rabbit], cat and fox.

Item 10. That esquires and all manner of gentlemen, under the estate of knight, which have no land nor rent to the value of 100 pounds by year, shall not wear cloth costing more than 4½ marks for the whole cloth ... and that they wear no cloth of gold, nor silk nor silver, nor no manner of clothing embroidered, ring, button, nor owche of gold ... nor no manner of fur ... and apparel without any turning up or purfle [ornamental border]. But that esquires that have land or rent to the value of 200 marks by year and above, may take and wear cloths of the price of 5 marks, and cloth of silk and of silver and other apparel reasonably garnished of silver. Their wives, daughters and children may wear fur turned up of miniver, without ermines, or any manner gemstones, but for their heads.

Item 11. Equates merchants, citizens and burgesses, as well within the city of London as elsewhere, who have goods worth 500 pounds with esquires and gentlemen worth 100 pounds. Merchants, etc. worth 1000 pounds equate with esquires and gentlemen worth 200 pounds.

Item 12. Knights worth £200 may wear cloth worth 6 marks but may not wear cloth of gold nor mantles nor gowns furred with miniver nor of ermines ... But that all knights and ladies, which have land or rent over the value of 400 marks by the year, to the sum of 1000 pounds, shall wear at their pleasure, except ermines and letuses, [a milk-white fur but I cannot discover the origin] and apparel of pearls and gemstones, but only for their heads.

Item 14. That carters, ploughmen, drivers of the plough, oxherds, cowherds, shepherds ... and all other keepers of beasts, threshers of corn, and all manner of people of the estate of a groom, attending to husbandry, and all other people that have not forty shillings of goods, nor chattels, shall not take nor wear no manner of cloth, but blanket, and russet wool of 12 pence; and shall wear the girdles of linen according to their estate; and that they come to eat and drink in the manner as pertaineth to them, and not excessively. And it is ordained, that if any wear or do contrary to any of the points aforesaid, that he shall forfeit against the king all the apparel that he hath so worn against the form of this ordinance.

HAUTE COUTURE

Luxurious clothes were one of the pleasures of the rich and a recognised mark of their status, so the complaints, usually made by churchmen, against dressing too extravagantly and spending too much money on high fashion weren't taken seriously. Christine de Pisan does her best to explain:

They [women] should especially avoid two things that, although quite common in other places, stem from the great pride that infects many women. As we are now concerned with that subject, and as those vices and faults can present a great danger to their souls and are not good or becoming even to the body, we will mention them. The first item is the very extravagant head-dresses and gowns that some women wear, and the other is the jostling that goes on when they try to get in front of each other at public functions.

Regardless, the great lords and ladies dressed themselves and their children as gorgeously as they could afford. During Eleanor de Montfort's lifetime, King Edward I had his children wearing caps of peacock feathers, gilded buttons – both for their clothes and the saddles of their horses – and gloves with the royal arms embroidered on them. Heavy gloves were used by labourers for all kinds of rough work, but elegant gloves were a mark of the rich and often given as presents, a tradition which continued at least until Elizabethan times. The Countess Eleanor bought a dozen pairs at one time for herself and her daughter at the very reasonable price of one penny a pair. A common present at any level of medieval society was a robe, although the term usually meant a tunic, a super tunic and a cloak. Such a gift would suit either a man or a woman as the basic elements were the same, although the cut would be different. The choice of materials used to make the clothes would then be determined by the recipient's place in society. As an example, Alice of Godstow was given a tunic, super tunic, a cloak with a hood and a furred coverlet, all of russet, as well as a coverlet of rabbit skins and a white counterpane of linen. This was a generous gift, but was made of cloth and furs worn only by the poor. In contrast, at Christmas 1238, King Henry III gave his sister, Eleanor, a piece of gold baudekin cloth, enough for a robe with a super tunic to be lined and trimmed with miniver.

There were three important types of material in use, which were wool, silk and linen. The woollen cloths were used most and English produce was the best. The elegant silks worn by the rich were imported from France, from the East and especially from Italy. Finally, some linens were imported from France, the Low Countries – 'diaper', which was of high quality and used for the best table linen, literally meant 'd'Ypres' – and some were made in England. The quality ranged from the finest 'sindon', which seems to have been a lawn or delicate muslin, to the coarse and ever-useful canvas.

Certain English towns had a special reputation for certain kinds of woollen cloth. The scarlets of Lincoln were the finest of all, having all the prestige of a designer label. However, scarlet referred to the kind of cloth, *not* to the colour – scarlet could be had in a variety of colours, though these were often shades of red, which may explain the origins of the confusion. Perse was another good quality woollen cloth, usually dyed a fine deep blue.

The actual brightness of the colours of medieval cloth is, of course, impossible to prove now. Some vegetable dyes, such as woad for blue and weld for yellow, may have tended to be muddy and uneven, especially on cheap cloth that had not been properly prepared for dyeing. However, reds, such as crimson, vermilion and 'grain', made from the *coccus* insects, and purple, prepared from the secretions of the sea mollusc *murex*, certainly were brilliant. The wealthier members of society could afford to buy the finest fabrics and, in the Middle Ages, this meant those with the brightest colours. Russets and burels were the coarsest and cheapest woollen cloths, worn mainly by the poor and distributed as charitable alms by the rich. However, the russets made in Colchester gained a rather better reputation and were sometimes worn by the wealthy, recently widowed – their version perhaps of sackcloth and ashes. Really coarse woollen cloths, like 'blanchet' or blanket, were used exactly for that purpose, for bed-coverings, although the poor might wear such cloth as a winter cloak.

Silks were imported and, therefore, most expensive and primarily used for church vestments and royal robes. Silken cloths, such as baudekin and samite, were always rare and very costly. The Italian weavers of Lucca had a flourishing industry in the thirteenth century, to be succeeded by the Florentines. They could imitate all the Oriental stuffs and their products could be bought at the great fairs held in Champagne, as well as from the merchants of London and Paris. Baudekin derived its name from Baghdad where it was made. It was often brocaded with gold and decorated with designs or figures. Samite was of Greek origin, although the Arabs and the Cypriots learned the secrets of its manufacture. Sendal was a type of taffeta that could vary greatly in quality and was used for banners and even tents. Damask, called after Damascus where it was made, is the only name still familiar to us today. It meant then, as now, a heavy cloth with designs woven into the body of the fabric. Camlet was another imported cloth, not silk this time, but woven from camel hair or goat hair, especially the very fine goat hair from Asia Minor. It had a long, velvety nap and was used by the wealthy for their winter robes – today's equivalent is probably cashmere.

EVERYDAY CLOTHES

For most folk, the basic cloth used for underwear was linen, although the quality could vary enormously. Apart from household linens for tablecloths and napkins, sheets and pillow slips, it was used for head coverings, underwear and aprons. Men wore 'drawers', which were like baggy boxer shorts with a drawstring; women wore a shift from neck to ankle but, it used to be thought, no bra or knickers. That was until fifteenth-century underwear – 'breast-bags' and tie-at-the-hip briefs – were discovered at Lengberg Castle in Austria in 2008. At the time of writing, the question as to whether the briefs were worn by a man or a woman is still being investigated and DNA tests to determine this have proved inconclusive, sadly. Personally, I think women would have greatly appreciated the convenience of knickers, especially once a month.

On top of their shift, women wore a tunic, or kirtle, a garment like a long shirt with long, quite fitted sleeves in the woman's case, which slipped over the head with a slit at the neck. This slit might be laced across or, more properly for ladies, fastened with a brooch befitting the wearer's status. The kirtle was held in place by a narrow belt or girdle, again suited to the wearer's place in society. Lacing itself was a crucial matter; it had to be done horizontally wherever it showed. This was being 'straight-laced'; if you cross-laced for quickness, you ran the risk of being reckoned a prostitute! Likewise, tying the bow had to be done with a single loop for lay men and women – double loop bows were for clerical persons only.

Over the kirtle went the super tunic or surcoat which was usually a little shorter (though fashions varied) with wide, loose sleeves and frequently lined with fur.

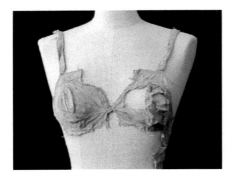

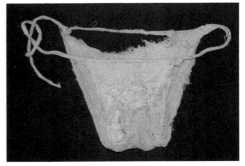

Above: Underwear found at Lengberg Castle, Austria. (Archaeological Institute, Innsbruck University)

Left: Lady with a lute. (MS Yates Thompson 32 f. 14, British Library – Marginalia, Charles the Bold and his court, *Chroniques abrégées des Anciens Rois et Ducs de Bourgogne*, Bruges, 1485)

Occasionally, perhaps for warmer weather, the surcoat could be sleeveless. Over this would go the mantle, made from an almost circular piece of cloth, fastened at the neck with a brooch or chain. It too was lined with fur to provide insulation against the cold and damp. This was the basic outfit, the whole ensemble being termed a 'robe', for women throughout the medieval period.

Then there were the vagaries of fashion. Over time, necklines dropped and rose again, as did hemlines. Sleeves became loose and flowing, then tightly fitted with a turned back cuff to show the fur lining, then cut away altogether in the sideless surcote. Waistlines, which, for much of the Middle Ages were at the hips with girdles hanging low, rose at the end of the fifteenth century as high as possible with broad belts being worn to accentuate the tiny waist and support the bust. However, fashions changed and the medieval lady always had to look her best, as much to demonstrate her husband's social standing as to be an ornament on his arm.

Women and the Church

During the Middle Ages, women were a subject of great confusion for the Church. Were they to be treated as the absolute inferiors of men or equal in the sight of God? Were they basically good or evil creatures? Today, it is difficult for us to take such questions seriously and even during the medieval period, it is doubtful that the average man or woman gave these issues much thought, unless as ammunition for a heated domestic argument. However, for the Church, the question of its attitudes towards women was a problem. The two extremes of these views of the feminine gender were represented by the images of Eve – the supreme temptress of mankind – and Mary – so perfect that she was the mother of God.

It had all begun back in Roman times, in the first century AD, when the upper classes in Roman society had adopted quite extreme negative attitudes towards women and sex. St Paul, writing at the time, had taken on the contemporary view of women as being totally subordinate to men and his words have been recorded in the New Testament, with such anti-feminine statements as, 'I would that all men were as I myself; it is good not to touch a woman', and, 'Wives, submit yourselves unto your husbands, as unto the lord'.

The first statement was to encourage celibacy, which St Paul saw as a state

Two nuns at the Battle of Bosworth re-enactment, 2014. (Pat Patrick)

of perfection, though quite how he expected the human race to continue if all men subscribed to the condition, he never explained. The second was a statement that all men could support wholeheartedly though, naturally, their wives were less inclined. However, on the whole, unfortunately for women, it was St Paul's command that prevailed in Church doctrine:

> And do you not know that you are Eve? ... You are the gate of the devil, the traitor of the tree, the first deserter of Divine Law; you are she who enticed the one whom the devil dare not approach [Adam]; you broke so easily the image of God, man; on account of the death you deserved, even the Son of God had to die.

This piece of invective was written by Tertullian, an early churchman who was nonetheless hypocrite enough to be married and refer to his wife as 'my beloved companion in the Lord's service'. However, the issue was always confusing. On the whole, women were thought of as having such limited mental capacity that education was likely to overtax them, yet, as in the example above, a women was able to tempt Adam to stray where the Devil could not succeed, so clever was she with her womanly wiles. This paradox is shown clearly in the writings of Salimbene, a Franciscan friar, whose confusion is more than evident: 'Woman, glittering mud, stinking rose, sweet venom ... a weapon of the devil, expulsion from Paradise, mother of guilt'. Compare this to a work by Marbode, an eleventh-century Bishop of Rennes, who clearly takes a far more charitable view of women: 'Of all the things that God has given for human use, nothing is more beautiful or better than the good woman'. He then cites the roles of comforter, mother, cook, housewife, spinner and weaver, declares that the worst woman who ever lived does not compare with Judas and the best man does not equal Mary and names a roll of honour of women from the Old Testament and the early Christian saints. Even more charitable in his outlook was the thirteenth-century Dominican master-general, Humbert de Romans:

> Note that God gave women many prerogatives, not only over other living things, but even over man himself, and this (i) by nature; (ii) by grace; and (iii) by glory.

> (i) In the world of nature she excelled man by her origin, for man He made of vile earth, but woman He made in Paradise. Man He formed of slime, but woman of man's rib. She was not made of a lower limb of man – as, for example, of his foot – lest man should esteem her his servant, but from his midmost part, that he should hold her to be his fellow, as Adam himself said: 'The woman whom Thou gavest as my helpmate.'

> (ii) In the world of grace she excelled man ... We do not read of any man trying to prevent the Passion of Our Lord, but we do read of a woman who tried – namely, Pilate's wife, who sought to dissuade her husband from so

great a crime ... Again, at His Resurrection, it was to a woman He first appeared – namely, to Mary Magdalen.

(iii) In the world of glory, for the king in that country is no mere man but a mere woman is its queen. It is not a mere man who is set above the angels and all the rest of the heavenly court, but a mere woman. Thus is woman's nature in Our Lady raised above man's in worth and dignity and power; and this should lead women to love God and to hate evil.

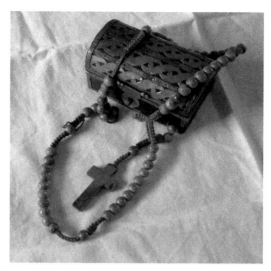

Wooden rosary and reliquary. (Glenn Mount)

The Dominican friars were, as churchmen, more sympathetic towards women than most. St Dominic, their Spanish founder in the early thirteenth century, thought it worthwhile to instruct women in religious matters and is believed to have invented the rosary to assist them in private prayer – a new innovation in religion at the time that was accompanied by the invention of books of hours for a similar purpose.

THE DEPICTION OF WOMEN IN RELIGION

So, at the two extremes, the Church found two perfect symbols: the shallow temptress, Eve; and the immaculate and perfect Virgin Mary. Mary, the virgin mother of God, was venerated in the Middle Ages above all other saints, so much so that historians refer to the 'Cult of the Virgin' and more medieval churches in England were dedicated to St Mary than to any other saint. This veneration may have had two reasons. The rise of powerful kings across Europe was reflected in a new idea of queenship and the belief that the royal line could only come from women who were strong, pure and faultless, in the image of the Virgin as Queen of Heaven. Secondly, there already existed the far more ancient cult of worshipping an earth mother, the goddess who dominated pagan religion. Therefore, May, the first month of summer and the month associated with the earth mother, became the month of Mary for the Catholic Church. Mary was represented by the May Queen (who should always have been a virgin) who was wedded to the Green Man, the ancient fertility symbol of pre-Christian Europe – a nice amalgamation of pagan and Christian ideas, though it is doubtful that the Church wished to dwell too long on the image of their favourite saint losing her virginity to a pagan.

Above left: A young woman at the Battle of Tewkesbury re-enactment, 2014. (Pat Patrick)

Above right: Virgin Mary. (MS Royal 6E IX, f.5, British Library – Italy, *c.* 1335–40)

The cult of the Virgin intensified during the fourteenth and fifteenth centuries as the Church declared that Mary herself had been conceived without the stain of original sin (the doctrine of the Immaculate Conception), and that, rather than suffering death and decay, she was taken directly to heaven (the Assumption). Of course, these doctrines made it even more impossible for ordinary women to take the Virgin as the ideal role model that they should emulate.

The eleventh and twelfth centuries seem to have produced more than the normal number of women who, despite the ultimate impossibilities, did their best to match the perfection of St Mary. Christina of Markyate belonged to a wealthy family in Huntingdon but, despite her parents' intentions of marrying her off to a suitable young man, she wished to retain her virginity and made a solemn vow to do so. Unfortunately for Christina, she was beautiful and attracted the unwelcome attentions of Ranulf Flambard, the notorious adviser to King William Rufus, who had made him, most unsuitably, Bishop of Durham. His interest in their daughter spurred Christina's parents into pressing her into marriage and they finally succeeded in betrothing her to a wealthy young man of good family, though the bride firmly refused to consummate the marriage. Her parents tried their hardest to force her to accept the situation.

At a grand feast, Christina was required to serve the wine, a duty that involved taking off her mantle, tightening her gown and rolling up her sleeves. Thus revealed, her parents hoped the compliments she would receive on her beauty and the sips of wine that normally accompanied each cup poured would break down her resolution but Christina performed her office with icy detachment. Finally, they took her young husband into her bedchamber, hoping he could achieve the consummation and seal the marriage. However, Christina managed to dissuade him the first night and then to evade him. Rather than support the young woman in her struggle to remain chaste, the local clergy rebuked her for failing to obey her parents' wishes, not wishing to offend such powerful patrons as the Markyate family.

The biography of Christina's life – a book commissioned by the Abbot of St Albans and written at the abbey – describes these events in emotional detail and emphasises that her family recognised their daughter's beauty, intelligence and practical ability. They were eager for her worldly success as it would enrich and ennoble herself and them and all her relatives as well. They couldn't understand nor accept a daughter who insisted on choosing her own path in life instead of meekly abiding by their wishes. In a vivid picture of domestic violence, the biography tells how her mother pulled her hair out and beat her. Her father was so angry he stripped her down to her shift, took away the keys he had given her, which means that he removed her responsibilities in the household, and – until restrained by a kindly guest – was ready to drive her out of the house on a winter's night.

Christina finally fled from her family's rage, took shelter with a recluse and was later taken under the protection of a hermit. After living for some years as a recluse herself, Christina took her monastic vows, becoming the head of a small Benedictine priory at Markyate where women, inspired by her story, gathered around her to form a small community.

CHAUCER'S PRIORESS – MADAME EGLENTYNE AND HER KIND

Here is Geoffrey Chaucer's rather cynical description of a prioress, one among his pilgrims riding to Canterbury. This woman was anything but a religious paragon:

> Ther was also a Nonne, a Prioresse,
> That of her smyling was ful simple and coy;
> Hir grettest ooth was ne but by seynt Loy;
> And she was cleped [called] madame Eglentyne .
> … But, for to speken of hir conscience,
> She was so charitable and so pitous,
> She wolde wepe, if that she sawe a mous
> Caught in a trap, if it were deed or bledde.
> Of smale houndes had she, that she fedde
> With rosted flesh, or milk and wastel-breed [fine bread].
> But sore weep she if oon of hem were deed,
> Or if men smoot it with a yerde smerte [stick, pain]:

And al was conscience and tendre herte.
Ful semely hir wimpel pinched was [pleated];
Hir nose tretys [well fashioned]; her eyen greye as glas;
Hir mouth ful smal, and ther-to softe and reed;
But sikerly [certainly] she hadde a fair foreheed ;
It was almost a spanne brood [broad], I trowe [believe];
For, hardily [scarcely], she was nat undergrowe.
Ful fetis [well made] was hir cloke, as I was war .
Of smal coral aboute hir arm she bar
A peire of bedes [rosary], gauded [beaded] al with grene;
And ther-on heng a broche of gold ful shene [very beautiful],
On which ther was first write a crowned A,
And after, Amor vincit omnia [Love conquers all]!

The prioress from the prologue to *The Canterbury Tales* sounds like quite an attractive lady – perhaps too much so to suit her religious vocation. Even her name, Madame Eglentyne, named after a wild rose, does not sound particularly religious. As specified by the Church, she wears a wimple but not a simple one: hers is pleated, and neither does it cover her forehead as it should. A lady's forehead was one of the few parts of her body which, though considered sexy, could be shown off in public, the fashion being to remove eyebrows and pluck hair from the front of the head to make the forehead as broad and high as possible. But a nun should keep her forehead covered by her wimple – clearly, for Madame Eglentyne, this was not the case. Chaucer's description of the lady's mouth – soft and red – may hint at the use of rouge.

Certainly, she is breaking the rules in keeping pets, which raises the question of how many other rules were broken in her priory. In the Middle Ages, every religious house was subject to regular 'visitations' by the bishop, to check that the rules were being adhered to. If they weren't, the head of the house could expect a stern warning and rather more frequent 'visitations' until the standard improved or else the ultimate punishment, the closure of the house. Bishops' visitation registers are very illuminating concerning the goings-on in abbeys and priories, because every member of the house, from highest to lowest, was invited to comment on the way things were run. The bishop wanted to find out if the prioress was ruling well, the services were conducted properly, the finances were in good order and discipline was maintained. The occasion of the bishop's visitation was the opportunity to complain for any nun who was not happy. The nuns were always full of complaints and the tale-telling is almost unbelievable. This selection is taken from the register of Bishop Alnwick of Lincoln in the fifteenth century:

One nun had boxed her sister's ears, another had missed church, another entertained friends, another went out without permission, another had run away with a wandering lute player. The Prioress fares splendidly in her own room and never invites us; she has favourites and when she makes corrections she passes lightly over those whom she likes and speedily punishes those whom she dislikes. She is a fearful scold; she dresses more like a secular person than a nun, and wears rings and necklaces. She goes out riding to see her friends far too often and she is a very bad business woman. She has let the house get into debt and the church is falling about our ears. We don't get enough food and she hasn't given us any clothes for two years. She has sold woods and farms without your licence and she has pawned our best set of spoons. She never consults us on any business as she ought to do.

Also from the Visitations of the Bishop of Lincoln (Bishop Richard this time) come these excerpts from the register concerning Godstow Abbey, near Oxford, in 1434:

Also that the present bailiff of the monastery has no private conversation with any nun since he says that there is not any good woman in the monastery.

Also that there [should] be no parties or drinks after compline, but when it [compline] is over all the nuns go together to the dormitory and lie there the night other than the abbess, if [unless] she be infirm or impeded by strangers to the profit and honour of the monastery, and except the infirm who then shall be lying in the infirmary.

Monk and a nun. (MS Royal 10 E IV f. 181, British Library – the 'Smithfield Decretals', Tolouse, France, first quarter of the fourteenth century)

... And that no nun receive any secular [person] for any recreation in their rooms under threat of excommunication. For the scholars of Oxford say that they can have whatever entertainment with the nuns they wish to desire.

Also that neither the monastery gatekeeper nor any other secular person convey any presents, rewards, letters or tokens to any Oxford scholars or any other secular persons from the nuns.

From the register concerning Ankerwyke Priory:

Dame Alice Hubbard had abided there for four years in nun's habit and had gone away in apostasy and married one Sutton, a blood relative of Master Richard Sutton, steward of Syon. She lives with him in adultery in Sutton's part of the world.

From an Episcopal Court Book for the Diocese of Lincoln:

Dame Katherine, prioress of Littlemore, appeared in person and was examined on various articles, some made against her on oath, others made by her on oath on the gospels.

To the first article she replied and acknowledged that as prioress she was subject to the jurisdiction of the Bishop of Lincoln.

To the second article she says that seven years ago she was known carnally and made pregnant by one Richard Hues, by whom, she claimed, she had a girl child. This witness confessed that she fed and cared for the child within the priory for three years up until the time of the child's death. She says further that Richard Hues was domestic chaplain to the prioress serving in her own house and that for six months seven years ago he kept company with the prioress and held her in incestuous embrace for that six months.

To the third article she says that before and after the feast of the Purification of Mary last Richard was with this witness in the priory and resided there the whole time. This witness confessed that by admitting Richard to her house she had done wrong and set a bad example to her sisters, but she was not known carnally by him on that date.

To the fourth article she responded that Dame Juliana Wynter gave birth to a girl child in the said nunnery begotten by one John Wikesley, a servant in the house ... She replies to the fifth article and denies it.

To the sixth article she acknowledges that she lent Richard Hues a feather bed with a bolster, a pair of sheets, a surplice and a silver chalice, all of which items Richard still has in his possession.

To the seventh article she denies that she wasted the assets of the monastery. She says, however, that a hundred pounds would not suffice to make adequate repairs to the priory. The prioress finally submitted herself to correction by the lord bishop of Lincoln.

You have to wonder what punishment Richard Hues received, if any.

MARGERY KEMPE

Margery Kempe was born about 1373 into very comfortable circumstances. Her father, John Burnham, was a wealthy and successful businessman and a prominent citizen of King's Lynn, or Bishop's Lynn as it was then known. In the fourteenth century, Lynn was a busy, thriving port and Margery's father represented the town in Parliament between 1364 and 1384. He was also an alderman of the Guild of the Holy Trinity, a wealthy, prestigious and exclusive trade organisation in Lynn.

Margery tells us nothing at all about her childhood, but begins her dictated autobiography abruptly with her marriage and the birth of her first child. Her husband was John Kempe, also a merchant of Lynn but less prominent and successful than her father, as she frequently reminded him. He was to be a very good and kind husband to her, despite that. Childbirth was a dangerous time for women in those unsanitary days and the birth of Margery's first child was traumatic. She was ill throughout the pregnancy and her labour was dreadful, causing her a physical and emotional crisis. Fearing she was dying, a priest was sent for to hear her confession but when she began to confess what had been troubling her for ages, he rushed her and interrupted. After that she would say no more to him but was 'tormented by demons', she said, for eight months after. As she tells us in her narrative (always referring to herself in the third person),

> She would have killed herself many times, as they [the demons] stirred her to, and would have been damned with them in hell. To witness this, she bit her own hands so violently that the scars could be seen for the rest of her life; and also she pitilessly tore the skin of her body near her heart with her nails, for she had no other weapon, and she would have done something even worse, if she had not been tied up and forcibly restrained both night and day.

What the terrible sin was that she couldn't confess, she doesn't say, but from other evidence in her story it seems it was of a sexual nature. The Middle Ages was not a period known for the humane treatment of the mentally ill and it says much for her husband's love and kindness that he kept her at home and had her constantly watched over. Then, one day, Margery had a vision – Jesus, garbed in purple silk, came and sat at her bedside and asked her, 'Daughter, why have you forsaken me, for I have never forsaken you?'

After that, she was cured and able to live normally again, grateful to God for restoring her sanity but by no means ready to give up worldly pleasures. She took delight in shocking people with her latest fashion in 'slashed' hoods and cloaks where the top layer of cloth was slit to reveal a contrasting colour beneath. Her husband told her she should dress more moderately and be less proud in her ways but she told him firmly that

> she came from a worthy family; he should never have married her ... and therefore she would keep up the honour of her family, whatever anyone said.

Margery candidly confesses that she was incredibly jealous if any of her neighbours were as well dressed as she was – she had not learnt her lesson, but God had not finished with her yet.

She decided to go into business for herself, not because the family needed the money – they didn't – but in order to have her own money to spend on clothes. She became a brewster and was very successful for three years but then, suddenly, the business failed – whatever she did, the ale was awful. She saw this as God's doing, in order to humble her pride, so she gave up brewing and bought a horse-mill to make money grinding people's corn. However, the rumour began that neither man nor beast would work for her because she was cursed.

> Then this creature, seeing all these adversities coming upon her from every side, thought they were the scourges of our Lord, punishing her for her sin. Then she asked God for mercy, and forsook her pride and her covetousness, and her desire for worldly reputation, and did great bodily penance, and began to enter the way of everlasting life.

From this time on, Margery was convinced that everything that happened to her was arranged by God to contribute to her personal salvation so she welcomed every experience of suffering and fear. One night, she was granted a vision of heaven itself and was so overcome that she wept copious and noisy tears – loud, hysterical and incessant weeping was to become a feature of her future devotions, something that drove her family to distraction and thoroughly annoyed the neighbours. She also gave herself up to fasting, keeping long vigils and secretly wearing a hair shirt. Even her husband never knew about the shirt, despite the fact they still shared a bed and, during the first twenty years of their marriage, she bore him fourteen children. It was the joys of sex that she intended to forfeit next in her quest for salvation and badgered her husband to give up his conjugal rights.

It was not until 1413, after many spiritual shortcomings and temptations, that Margery finally succeeded in persuading her husband that he should allow her to take a vow of chastity. Once free of that which bound her to marriage, she took up a life of pilgrimage. Her father died in 1413, leaving her sufficient money that she could afford to travel to Jerusalem, though her fellow pilgrims did not relish her company with so much hysterical weeping and wailing and tried everything to get her to leave them, making her look a fool at every opportunity. God had promised her she would make the journey safely and return, also that any Englishman accompanying her would not die. When some of her shipmates on the voyage fell ill, Margery was suddenly their guarantee of recovery and was accepted. Her later pilgrimages included Rome and St James of Compostella in northern Spain where, though destitute, the Lord told her not to worry and she was provided for.

The early fifteenth century was the time of Lollardy in England and, back home, Margery found herself accused of heresy on two occasions, but after she came before the Archbishop of York for examination, he declared the charges were nonsense and sent her home to Lynn. There, her husband John, now over sixty, had fallen down the stairs and suffered serious head injuries; Margery was blamed for having neglected him. She cared for him, incontinent and increasingly senile, until he died in 1431. Then, at the age of sixty, she set off on her travels again, this time to Germany, to see the relics in various churches from Danzig to Aachen. When she returned to Lynn in 1435, she persuaded a priest to write a book of her life. He was only just starting volume two in April 1438, complaining that it was difficult, but Margery insisted that he continue, saying that God would keep his eyesight keen. Also in 1438, Margery was admitted as a member of the Guild of Holy Trinity in Lynn, an honour that shows the townspeople had come to feel proud of their local mystic.

There are no further records of her life and we don't know when she died but, when her story was reprinted in 1512, the introduction refers to her as a 'devout anchoress'. If this was true, then she had spent her final years as a recluse, having given up her travels and dedicated herself exclusively to God in a cell attached to her local church, St Margaret's, in Lynn. We will, however, probably never know for certain.

CECILY NEVILLE, DOWAGER DUCHESS OF YORK

Cecily Neville was born in May 1415 (the year of the Battle of Agincourt), the youngest daughter of Ralph Neville, Earl of Westmorland, and his second wife, Joan Beaufort, an illegitimate child of John of Gaunt and his mistress, Katherine Swynford, though the children of this union had been legitimised. All the Neville-Beaufort offspring, of whom there were many, made prestigious marriages and Cecily's was the most excellent match. The Earl of Westmorland purchased the wardship of the orphaned Duke of York for 3,000 marks from the Crown and, when Cecily was nine, she and young Richard, Duke of York, were married in 1424.

The Duke of York had a strong claim to the throne and, when King Henry VI became mentally incapacitated in 1453, the duke staked that claim. The result was the Wars of the Roses. For the duke, the war ended at his death at the Battle of Wakefield in 1460 but, for his family, the conflict went on. The widowed duchess would see two of her sons wear the crown of England: the eldest as Edward IV; the youngest as Richard III; but what effect did these traumas have on the Lady Cecily herself?

Known as the 'Rose of Raby' for her beauty and 'Proud Cis' for her haughtiness, she preferred to be known after 1461 as the 'King's Mother, Duchess of York'

Raby Castle, Durham. (John Clive Nicholson)

and second lady in the land after the queen – a position that irked her because Edward's wife came of less elevated stock. Perhaps because remarriage could only reduce her status, Cecily never sought another husband but settled for grand and gracious widowhood. In 1480, she and her widowed sister, Anne, Dowager Duchess of Buckingham, took the vows of the Benedictine Order at Northampton. However, Cecily didn't retire altogether from the world, nor did she lead a life of seclusion in a religious house. Instead, she took up semi-permanent residence at her secluded castle of Berkhampstead and withdrew, as far as possible, from all worldly pleasures and occupations. She never left the castle except for the rare occasions when her duties as mother to a king demanded it.

Within its walls she lived a severe and austere life as dictated by the Benedictine Rule, her days dominated by hours of private prayer and meditation. Between 7 a.m. and 8 p.m., she heard three services of matins, three low masses and three evensongs, some in private, others in chapel. It was the hours of meditation and the dedication she showed in her studies, however, that made her piety stand out, so much so that once Proud Cis was considered the most saintly lay person of her generation.

Cecily ate her meals in silence while a priest read aloud from some appropriate sacred text and, most unusually, she owned books on spiritual mysticism which she kept by her in her chamber. They included some advanced works of great depth and complexity, such as those by St Catherine of Sienna and St Bridget of Sweden, as well as *The Booke of Gostlye Grace*, a translation of the Visions of St Mechtild of Hackeborn. For a laywoman like Cecily to voluntarily read them every day and understand the texts well enough to discuss them at length with her priests shows great devotion and intellect. In an age when women's education in such matters was so sparing, Cecily's piety must have been remarkable and worthy of comment.

PIETY IN MEDIEVAL WILLS

Wills are an excellent guide to the feelings of ordinary laywomen regarding their local church. Some of the bequests they make suggest that, as was the ideal in the medieval period, nothing was too good for God, and some items on the church inventories must have been incredibly valuable, as we can see from these few examples from St Ewen's in Bristol in 1455:

> Also, a pair of vestments of red damask of the gift of Elizabeth Scharpe with other things thereto according.

> Also, one coat to St Katherine [an image of] of satin of Cypress with one piece of coral capped with silver of the gift of Katherine Gylys.

> Receipts of bequests and gifts to the Cross: of Isabel Gyllard, one pot sold for 4s. 10d.
> Also of Maud Hopkyn, 6s. 8d.
> Also of Dame Margaret Leche, 12d.
> … of Agnes, George Roche's wife, 3s. 4d.

> Also of Alice Sylkwoman, one ring of silver weighing a half quarter and one farthing gold weight.
> Also of Lucy Thomas, one ounce of silver.

> Also of the executors of Edith Blays, one spoon weighing one ounce.
> Also Dame Margaret Leche, a half ounce and one farthing gold weight.
> Also of Joan Hoper, widow, one ounce, a half and two pennies weight.

Thomas Bardolffe, a woolman of York, in his will dated 1432, left money to Margaret Erysacre 'to go on pilgrimage for me to Canterbury on her own feet, 13s 4d.'

In 1388, Cecily Giry of York left a charitable bequest in her will that,

> I will that the three feather beds with the sheets pertaining to them in the guest chamber remain there to serve as a hospice for the needy.

Agnes Poost, a widow from Doncaster, states in her will,

> Also I bequeth all my wood and coals to be divided among poor people hastily after my death.

As you can see, it was common in wills to leave cloth, books, silverware and money to the church. Alms for the poor were also considered a good investment to ensure the safe passage of the deceased's soul through Purgatory. In her will of 1485, Katherine Mason leaves a diaper tablecloth and 13s 4d to the church of St Magnus in London and 6s 8d to the church of St Olave. Despite living in London at the time of drawing up her will and with her husband's family coming from Lavenham in Suffolk, it seems Katherine had connections with Shoreham in Kent. She leaves 53s 4d for the upkeep of the little bridge over the Darenth in Shoreham and 6s 8d for the poor of the village who have children. She also gives a further 6s 8d to church works there, in other words, to maintain the fabric of the church. Incidentally, paying for the maintenance of roads and bridges was also seen as an act of charity, benefitting the community as a whole.

Sadly though, not every woman was as pious as those mentioned above. Let us end with a couple of examples from the Court of the Archdeacon of Buckingham in 1489:

At Penn. Isabel Bovyngton does not keep the Sabbath. She appeared and confesses the article and is beaten thrice through the church and dismissed.

Thomas, John and William, the sons of the same Isabel for like cause. They appeared and confessed guilt. They did penance and were dismissed.

At Langley. Joan Mason and Thomas Mason – because they do not keep the Sabbath holy. They are let off and dismissed.

Epilogue

Although we have seen that life for medieval women was nothing like our experiences today, their emotions and outlook were not so different from our own in the twenty-first century. Technology, life style and expectancy have all changed dramatically, but human nature remains the same. Many women still have to juggle family and household needs with duties outside the home, much as their forebears did over five hundred years ago. The twenty-first century has its share of Dame Elizabeth Cooks, Noah's wives and Lady Eleanor de Montforts, doing the best for their children, being cantankerous, or more than capable, although perhaps the extraordinarily devout Christina Markyates are few these days. We still worry about the family's health, minor legal wrangles, what to wear and what to have for dinner and, as the Tudor writer, Thomas Tusser, reminded us at the beginning, 'Housewives' affairs have never an end.'

And I think we will agree with him there.

Marriage. (MS Lansdowne 451 f. 230, British Library – Pontifical; Tabula, England, first quarter of the fifteenth century)

Acknowledgements

I wish to thank Dr Heather Falvey who so kindly edited the first edition of this book. It was originally compiled as a set of notes for my students who wanted a record of my course *The Role of Medieval Women* back in 2007, but told me they couldn't write fast enough or remember it all, even though the course was just for enjoyment without any test or examination at the end. Any errors which may have crept in to the text since then are down to my addition of new material and updates in research.

I am grateful to Nicola Gale at Amberley Publishing who had the idea of turning that modest little book into a colourful, larger format, soft cover version.

Many thanks to Pat Patrick, freelance photographer at Owl & Trig Pillar (Blandford) Productions, who kindly provided access to his extensive collection of re-enactment and living history photographs and agreed for me to use these freely within this book. Grateful thanks also to the fraternity of re-enactment and living history participants who entertain the public at events every week up and down the country.

As always, Glenn has been a tower of strength and inspiration, tracking down suitable images and photographs. Without his work in compiling and indexing the original self-published version, there would not have been a book at all.

Bibliography

MEDIEVAL HOUSEWIVES

Alexander, M., *The Canterbury Tales: Illustrated Prologue* (Scala Books)
Black, M., *The Medieval Cookbook* (British Museum Press, 1992)
Hammond, P., *Food and Feast in Medieval England* (Sutton, 1993)
Hanawalt, B. A., *Growing up in Medieval London* (Oxford University Press, 1995)
Power, E., *The Goodman of Paris* (Folio Society Edition, 1992)
Will of Ellen Langwith (Archbishop of Canterbury's Probate Register 1479–86)

WOMEN IN TRADE

Britnell, R. (ed.), *Daily Life in the Late Middle Ages* (Sutton, 1998)
Sutton, A., and P. Hammond, *The Coronation of Richard III* (Gloucester, 1983)
Thrupp, S. L., *The Merchant Class of Medieval London* (Ann Arbor Paperbacks, 1989)
Vale, J., *The Politics of Fifteenth Century England, John Vale's Book* (Sutton, 1995)
Wardrobe Accounts of Edward IV (Facsimile Edition)
Will of Dame Elizabeth Coke (Archbishop of Canterbury's Probate Register 1479–86)

PEASANT WOMEN

Backhouse, J. (ed.), *The Luttrell Psalter* (The British Library, 1989)
Cruden, R. P., *History of Gravesend and the Port of London* (Johnstone and Barrett, 1843)
Ziegler, P., *The Black Death* (Penguin, 1982)

MEDIEVAL LADIES

Coss, P., *The Lady in Medieval England 1000–1500* (Sutton, 1998)
Goodman, J., *Chivalry and Exploration* (Boydell and Brewer, 1998)
Labarge, M. W., *A Baronial Household of the Thirteenth Century* (Harvester, 1980)
Martin, P., *Chaucer's Women* (Macmillan Press, 1996)
Rous, J., *The Rous Roll* (Sutton, 1980)

WOMEN'S DRESS AND FASHION

Cunnington, P., *Costume* (Black, 1966)
University of Innsbruck http://www.uibk.ac.at/urgeschichte/projekte_forschung/
    textilien-lengberg/medieval-lingerie-from-lengberg-castle-east-tyrol.html

WOMEN AND THE CHURCH

Chamberlayne, J., 'A Paper Crown: The Titles and Seals of Cecily, Duchess of
    York' in *The Ricardian,* Vol. X, no. 133 (June 1996)
Halsted, C., *Richard III* (Sutton, 1977)
Martin, P., *Chaucer's Women* (Macmillan Press, 1996)
Power, E., *Medieval People* (Folio Society Edition, 1999)
Will of Katherine Mason (Archbishop of Canterbury's Probate Register 1479–86)

Index